Cheryl,

Congratu[lations] [on your]
up-coming nuptials. [May God]
bless you as you grow in
Christ.

In Christ,
Mary

MW01383031

Removing the Dirt in the Church

A Twenty-First Century Call to Holiness

Mary E. Smith

Copyright © 2022 Mary E. Smith.

All rights reserved. No part of this book may be used or reproduced by any means, graphic, electronic, or mechanical, including photocopying, recording, taping or by any information storage retrieval system without the written permission of the author except in the case of brief quotations embodied in critical articles and reviews.

This book is a work of non-fiction. Unless otherwise noted, the author and the publisher make no explicit guarantees as to the accuracy of the information contained in this book and in some cases, names of people and places have been altered to protect their privacy.

WestBow Press books may be ordered through booksellers or by contacting:

WestBow Press
A Division of Thomas Nelson & Zondervan
1663 Liberty Drive
Bloomington, IN 47403
www.westbowpress.com
844-714-3454

Because of the dynamic nature of the Internet, any web addresses or links contained in this book may have changed since publication and may no longer be valid. The views expressed in this work are solely those of the author and do not necessarily reflect the views of the publisher, and the publisher hereby disclaims any responsibility for them.

Cover designed by Christina Dixon.

"Scripture quotations taken from the (NASB®) New American Standard Bible®, Copyright © 1960, 1971, 1977, 1995 update by The Lockman Foundation. Used by permission. All rights reserved. www.lockman.org"

Scripture taken from the King James Version of the Bible.

Scripture taken from the New King James Version® Copyright © 1982 by Thomas Nelson. Used by permission. All rights reserved.

Scripture quotations taken from The Holy Bible, New International Version® NIV® Copyright © 1973 1978 1984 2011 by Biblica, Inc. TM. Used by permission. All rights reserved worldwide.

ISBN: 978-1-6642-5918-8 (sc)
ISBN: 978-1-6642-5917-1 (hc)
ISBN: 978-1-6642-5919-5 (e)

Library of Congress Control Number: 2022903604

Print information available on the last page.

WestBow Press rev. date: 04/26/2022

CONTENTS

Acknowledgments vii
Introduction ix

Part 1   The Christian Defined 1

What is a Christian? 1
Early Christians 2
Christianity Misconstrued 4
    Ignorant and Unstable 6
    Divided Disobedient.. 8
    Willful Disobedient 10
    Fearful and Unbelieving 12
    Condescending Prideful.. 14
    Counterfeit 16
Surrendered versus Unsurrendered Life 19
Self-Examination Time 23

Part 2   Down and Dirty 25

Biblical Characters 25
    Aaron 25
    Miriam 28
    Ten Spies 32
    Korah and Company 35
    Moses 38
    Achan 43
    Unnamed Man of God 46

Pharisee 50

Peter 52

Saul/Paul 55

Systemic Sin in Israel and the Church............................ 58

Shepherds of Israel 58

Sheep of Israel.. 62

Sin in the Church System 63

Part 3   God's Dirt Removal Plan...................................... 71

The Body of Christ 71

We're in This Together..74

My Survivor Story of Clergy Sexual Abuse..................... 79

Conclusion... 91

References 93

About the Author 95

ACKNOWLEDGMENTS

To God, my heavenly Father, thank you. For from you and through you and to you are all things. To you be the glory forever. Amen. Thank you for giving me parents who knew and loved you.

To Ray, my beloved husband and best friend. Thank you for your undying love and support through every hardship life has brought our way. Against all odds, we've faced everything together and have grown up together. I could not have written this book without you.

To my sons, Raymond, Joseph, and Timothy. What more can a mom ask for? To God be the glory for the exemplary men you have become! You have inspired my continued growth as a follower of Christ.

To Christina Dixon, thanks for holding my hand through this process. Your prayers, feedback, and accountability were invaluable helping me to finally get the book out of my head and onto the pages.

To Pat Hicks, and to the WestBow Press editing team, thank you for helping to polish the manuscript.

To Clotee Ware, my prayer partner for decades, your godly example of womanhood is inspiring. Thank you for praying for this project from conception to completion. To my other prayer warriors, too many to name, thank you. You know who you are. I love you all.

To my family and church family, previous and current, thank you for your prayers and encouragement.

INTRODUCTION

Most people don't like to hear bad news, but sometimes hearing bad news is necessary. It's reminiscent of news on TV. While there are many great things going on in the world, we hear mostly negative things on the news. Sometimes hearing the unpleasant things can be protective. If a hurricane is coming, we can take the appropriate action to secure our property and get to safety. We never wake up with the desire to find out a hurricane is coming our way. But if one is coming, we'd rather know in time to prepare than to be caught completely off guard. *Removing the Dirt in the Church* sounds the alarm that there are storms brewing in the church.

Importance of Calling Sin ... Sin

"Dirt" in the title of this book stands for sin. Sin is not a popular word in today's postmodern world. Relativism has made it inappropriate to call anyone's actions wrong. I mean, who am I to say that something is wrong? People have a right to do what they want as long as it isn't against the law, right? And if what one wants to do is against the law, and a lot of other people want to do it too, if they lobby hard enough, they can start a movement and change the law, right? In this democratic society, a lot of positive change has happened in the past because of this process. However, this book will examine sin, not from a relative or democratic point of view, but from God's perspective as written in his Word, the Bible. Specifically, we will address sin in the Christian church. Sin is any thought, word, attitude, or action that displeases God. We want to remove the dirt in the church because the church is meant to be salt and light, which reflects the holiness of God to the world.

"Church" in the title does not refer to the building where Christians meet to have worship services. The church is the universal collective group of people who have believed the gospel of Jesus Christ and have trusted in Christ as their Savior from sin, i.e., Christians. Individual Christians are to represent Christ in and to the world. It's not that Christians must do everything exactly right in order to be followers of Christ, but they have an observable lifestyle of faith and holiness lived in humble devotion to Christ and his teachings. Among the church are people who profess to be Christ followers, but their lives do not bear the fruit that demonstrates their union with Christ. These may be immature or carnal, or they may be counterfeit (i.e., fake—not Christians at all). There is hope for both.

Why

Many people have come to the church for solace and shelter from the storms of life only to find that the church is not exempt from devastating storms. We (God through me) will give hope to those who have been caught in a church storm. We will encourage the wounded to find a safe church fellowship where they can heal, grow, and contribute to the overall health of the church. We will speak to the individual who is in the church, but the church is not in them. We will encourage the reader to have realistic expectations of the local church and to explore how they can be used by God to make it better.

I am writing this book to encourage the church to accurately represent Christ. As someone who has been in the church all my life, I have seen many things! I've seen the good, the bad, and the ugly. I believe I've seen mostly God-honoring things. This book is not about those good, God-honoring things. It's about some things that need to change. I do not presume that I am the one who sets the standards. I do not. God's Word gives us the standard. This book will show some areas where we, as God's church, can do better. This is not a church-bashing book. It's a church-loving book for both the individual and the corporate level.

There are individuals in the church that give the church a bad name. These individuals live lifestyles that say anything but "Be imitators of me, just as I also am of Christ" (1 Corinthians 11:1). We all can afford to do better. This book will encourage us all to do just that. We will observe some of the failures of biblical characters and demonstrate that we are in good company. If there was hope for them, there is hope for us today. But I have bad news. There are big systemic problems. This book addresses the sad, and albeit recurrent systemic, problems of clergy sexual and financial abuse, hypocrisy, and partiality in the church.

Finally, I will share my survivor story of clergy sexual abuse, what I learned, and how God grew my faith as a result. The fact that there is dirt in the church is no surprise to God. He knows. He sees, and he has a dirt removal plan.

PART 1

The Christian Defined

What is a Christian?

In this section, we will first examine what it means to be a Christian. We will then consider the beliefs and behaviors of early Christians. Finally, we will delve into various mindsets that fall short of Christian ideals, thus heaping dirt in the church.

The word *Christian* literally means a follower of Christ. From the Bible's perspective, a Christian is one who has acknowledged one's propensity to sin and need of the Savior. They have chosen by God's grace to turn away from their sin to God and trust in the sacrificial death and resurrection of Christ for cleansing from their sin and its eternal consequences to live in surrender to God and his will for their lives (repentance). They have believed the gospel—the death, burial, and resurrection of the Lord Jesus Christ (1 Corinthians 15:3–4). It is through their faith in Christ that Christians are saved from sin, receiving salvation. "For by grace you have been saved through faith; and that not of yourselves, it is the gift of God; not as a result of works, so that no one may boast" (Ephesians 2:8–9).

A Christian is someone who has been rescued from the slavery to sin and its punishment—death—to receive the gift of God—eternal life in Christ Jesus (Romans 6:23). The Bible teaches that "through one man [Adam] sin entered into the world, and death through sin, and so death spread to all men, because all sinned" (Romans 5:12). Because of Adam's sin, humankind was under a death sentence, but through the obedience of Christ, who never sinned, we can be made righteous and receive eternal

Removing the Dirt in the Church

life (Romans 5:19, 21). Christians believe and receive what Christ has done on their behalf, which they could not do for themselves. Christians are saved by faith in what Christ has done on their behalf, and they also live by faith (Romans 1:17). Christians are in a growing relationship with God, their heavenly Father; they are never alone and have unlimited access to God through prayer.

Early Christians

First-century Christians were excited to share their faith with others. In obedience to Christ, they were compelled to preach Christ regardless of personal cost. Identifying as Christian was looked upon by the religious leaders of the day as forsaking God and turning away from Judaism (Acts 5:17–18, 28). As a result, Christians were persecuted and often martyred (Acts 12:1–3). The early Christian church was made up of Jews who believed that Jesus was the promised Messiah. Having understood the Old Testament prophecies fulfilled by Christ and having witnessed Christ's death, burial, and resurrection, they gladly preached the good news of salvation through faith in Christ. They rejoiced and felt honored when persecuted for Christ's sake and persevered to the death (Acts 5:41–42). Unfortunately, one who is filled with hope, joy, and perseverance does not describe many who identify as Christian today.

Early Christians had the Old Testament but did not have the benefit of the complete Old Testament and New Testament at its beginning. Initially, Christians were centralized in Jerusalem. Persecution from unconverted Jews caused believers to be scattered, and they preached the gospel as they traveled. New churches were formed as a result. The apostles— eyewitnesses of the resurrected Christ—were used by the Holy Spirit to preach the gospel of Jesus Christ and to instruct the believers in these new churches. The Holy Spirit inspired letters to be written by some apostles to the first-century churches in various cities and to the Christian community at-large, which comprise three-quarters of the New Testament.

Only those who were convinced of the truth of the gospel dared to become Christians in the first century, and many were convinced (Acts 5:13). Acts 5:14 says, "And all the more believers in the Lord, multitudes of men and women, were constantly added to their number." They were

The Christian Defined

convinced for two reasons. First was persecution (Acts 8:1). Despite persecution, however, the early church continued to grow. Second was apostolic authority. The apostles' authority was confirmed as they were able to perform miracles, as did Christ (Acts 5:12). Miracles were also done by the Holy Spirit on their behalf. They were also spokesmen of the Holy Spirit's judgment to those who would lie or insincerely claim Christ (Acts 5:3–10; 8:14–24). The reverential fear of first-century Christians was very different from what we see in mainline Christianity today, especially in the United States.

> *Mature Christians have a hope within that enables them to persevere through trials with joy.*

Many Christians today, sadly, are not clear on the issue of holiness in the life of the believer. True Christians are new creations in Christ (2 Corinthians 5:17), and they are called to be salt and light in the world (Matthew 5:13–16). Jesus followers follow Jesus, and their lifestyle is not dictated by the world. Although we live in the world, Christians are not of the world. This distinction between living in and not being of the world does not mean that Christians are better than non-Christians. It means that Jesus is Lord of the Christian's life, and by the grace given to them by Christ, they live according to his will instead of their own will or the will of others (Romans 12:1–2). The Bible is their standard of faith and life, and ideally, they have disciplined themselves to study and rightly divide it. Through their study and practice of God's Word, they have learned who God is and what he is like. Mature Christians have a hope within that enables them to persevere through trials with joy. Even while expressing sorrow, they are assured by God's Word, the Bible, that they are not alone and that everything will work together for their good (Romans 8:28–39). They are empowered to live counterculturally and have pleasing Christ as their goal. But what exactly does it mean to be a Christian? How does it look as a lifestyle?

Removing the Dirt in the Church

Christianity Misconstrued

Some people consider themselves Christian because they live in the United States, because their parents claimed to be Christians, or because they attended church as children. They do not see Christianity as a relationship with God or as a lifestyle. In fact, many in the United States believe that all religions are equal and that it really does not matter which religion one chooses. Further investigation would reveal that many who claim to be Christian do not believe the same tenets that first-century Christians believed. There are Christian cults in our world.

Salvation from the power and penalty of sin through faith in the finished work of Jesus Christ, the Son of God, is the heart of the gospel message. The changed life of the Christian is like fragrance that is used to draw men unto Christ. The Bible teaches that God is impeccably holy and incapable of sin (Isaiah 6:3), and that man apart from God is bound to sin. The most righteous effort of the unregenerate is filthy and unacceptable to God (Isaiah 64:6). Man, because of the fall of Adam and Eve, was desperately lost in sin (Romans 5:12). So man's sinfulness separated him from his holy Creator. But God in his love for us sent his only Son as a perfect sacrifice for our sins (Romans 5:8). Christ purchased our salvation with his own precious blood on Calvary and rose again on the third day in victory over death, hell, and the grave. It is through faith in what Christ has done that we can be born again. Through Christ, fellowship with God and eternal life are gained. But each individual must accept and trust in what Christ has done on their behalf for them to be made right with God. This is what is meant by salvation, which results in an inward change that will be evident in how one who has been redeemed lives.

After salvation, we have a new nature and are spiritually alive. So now that we have a new nature, are we perfect? Are we sinless? God commands us in his Word to be holy. Would he command this if it were impossible to obey? Paul tells of a battle that rages in the Christian: the spirit against the flesh. In Romans 7, Paul tells of his personal struggle of doing what he hates and omitting what he loves. His desire was to do good, but he found himself doing evil. But he also thanked God that Christ is his deliverer at the end of the same chapter. In Romans 8, he reveals the secret of how he became victorious over that struggle. So had he reached perfection? Can

The Christian Defined

we reach perfection? Does God really expect perfection? In Matthew 5:48 he commands it, but does he expect it?

This is a very critical issue. If you're a Christian, you know that honestly you have not been perfect since your conversion. You haven't even been close! First John 1:8 tells us, "If we say that we have no sin, [or that we're perfect], we are deceiving ourselves and the truth is not in us." It only takes a glance to see that the church as a whole is far from the standard that God has in his Word. So again, does God really expect holiness and perfection?

Let's explore both sides. Say the answer is no. We know by the Word of God and by self-examination that we are not perfect and holy. Some would argue that God does not expect holiness and perfection because he made provisions for when we sin (see 1 John 2:1–2). Some people say, "God knew I was going to sin before I did, and he understands me."

God is omniscient and understands us, but does that excuse sin? God's provision for sin does not mean that he does not mind it. Yes, Christians can sin. That's a fact. God knew that (he knows everything) and made provisions for it. Knowing the fact that God made provisions for if we sin is like a healthy person knowing where the hospital is. He is assured that if he gets sick, he can be treated at the hospital and may recover. But it is foolish to have the attitude that says, "Because I live near a hospital, I won't take care of myself. I'll indulge in whatever I want, when I want, as long as I want or completely neglect my body, because I can get fixed up at the hospital."

Some professing Christians live like this. Since God forgives and remembers their sin no more, they can carelessly indulge in sin and please the flesh for as often and as long as they like, completely neglecting themselves spiritually. They seem to feel that they can do their own thing and go to heaven too. After all, God's love and grace is limitless! Their theme is "saved by the grace of God, not of works." That may be because they aren't even trying to obey.

On the other end of the spectrum, there are others who are very new to following Christ. They have a lot to learn, and, like a baby learning to walk, they may spend more time on the floor than actually taking steps. Their sin is not deliberate or premeditated. They just need to learn better before they can do better.

Removing the Dirt in the Church

Ignorant and Unstable

We will examine six different heart conditions with the accompanying attitudes, motives, or mindsets that people can have about sin. The first we'll call the ignorant and unstable. New Christians are often in this category. There is so much to learn about God and his will, which takes time. It is important in this stage that godly, mature Christians help disciple these baby Christians. They are to teach and model righteousness to these babes who may sin because they don't know any better. They can be like newborns, self-centered and dependent on others for their survival. In time they will learn to do better. They will learn to trust and obey God for themselves, study the Word for themselves, and even to confidently share their faith with others. Baby Christians can, however, experience a sudden radical change that testifies of Christ's presence and power in their lives. Therefore, it does not have to take a long time before change and growth can occur in the new convert.

In addition to new Christians, there are Christians who, although they may not be new to Christ, have misunderstandings about some vital truths. They believe lies. They can have the right motive and the right attitude, but they still sin because they have the wrong information.

Sometimes we can come to wrong conclusions because of our own limited experience. We may have a disproportioned view of God's expectations of us. For example, some may think that all God wants of us is church attendance and occasional giving to a worthy cause. That thinking puts God in a box that does not give him first place in the other areas of our lives. We may also have lopsided expectations of God. Some Christians may think that because they attend church and pray, God will make their lives problem free. Or they expect God to be their personal miracle worker who makes all things work out just as they'd like. We may fail to understand the factors that make it easy for us to sin. Doing A, which may not technically be a sin, will often lead to B, which definitely is a sin. For example, it is not technically a sin to go to a restaurant that serves alcohol with friends. But if a Christian who goes there with his friends ends up drunk, then he has sinned (Ephesians 5:18). We can better avoid sin when we understand the things that facilitate sin in our lives. Sin facilitators may vary from person to person.

The Christian Defined

On the other hand, this wrong information may be deliberately given by wolves in sheep's clothing who are looking for someone to victimize. The ignorant can be led into sin or baited and trapped by someone they trust as more mature in Christ than themselves. Therefore, it is so important for us to forsake immaturity, study for ourselves, and get to know God's voice for ourselves. We must learn to trust the Holy Spirit who now resides in us (Romans 8:9; 1 John 4:13). He is our resident teacher (John 16:13–14; 1 John 2:27). Even though he uses others to help us to grow, no one is to ever be a substitute for him. When babes, the misinformed, or the misled sin, there are still consequences. It is part of growing up. When you sin, you are harming yourself and others. Just as a loving parent gives consequences to discourage young ones from harming themselves, God does the same thing. He may not give the same discipline to the one who didn't know any better as he would to the one who knew better and yet did it anyway. But he will discipline them because he loves them (Hebrews 12:6).

The ignorant can be led into sin or baited and trapped by someone they trust as more mature in Christ than themselves.

Reflections

1. What, if anything, resonated with you from the section Ignorant and Unstable as an area that needs attention in your life?
2. Think of the past year. How would you or those Christians closest to you characterize your spiritual growth or knowledge and practice of biblical principles? Maturing? Vacillating? Stagnant?
3. If you are consistent in the biblical practice of your faith in Christ, who can you encourage to do the same? How will you encourage them?

Removing the Dirt in the Church

Prayer

Thank you, heavenly Father, for the people who have come along side me to help me grow in my faith. May I have an ever-growing desire for and the discipline to consistently take in the milk of your Word. Please teach me to learn to rightly discern your Word for myself and grow to help others to do the same. As I am able, give me a willingness to give of myself to mentor someone else in their walk with you. Shed your light on and correct any lies I may believe or areas of blindness I may possess. Thank you for the assurance that just as you began this work in me, you will perfect it until the day of Jesus Christ. Amen.

Divided Disobedient

The second attitude we will explore is the divided disobedient. In their minds they want to obey because they know that it's the right thing to do. In their hearts they still want to cling to their sin because they want to satisfy the flesh, now. The flesh will not go down without a fight. So this divided person considers, "How close can I get to the line without technically crossing over?" They initially may not understand that at the line of sin, there is a vacuum. If you get too close, it is as if the invisible forces of sin gain momentum and suddenly pull you over the line. They keep testing how far they can go, until they learn that you can't win with that strategy. They are often dismayed when they get pulled over the line because they truly did not intend to go that far. They don't want to have the consequences of disobedience but want their flesh to be soothed. They don't understand that there is only one way to deal with the flesh. Kill it! Don't kill your physical body but kill the ungodly desires that work in your body moving you to sin against God. In other words, we are to "consider the members of [our] earthly body as dead to immorality, impurity, passion, evil desire, and greed, which amounts to idolatry" (Colossians 3:5). Do not be deceived. Satan wants to get his foot in the door. If you give him an inch, he'll take a mile and more. As with the ignorant and unstable, whether it's intentional or not, for the divided disobedient there are

The Christian Defined

consequences for crossing the line of sin. God wants us all—heart, soul, mind, and strength. He will continue to deal with the divided until they love him with their whole being.

After looking at all God has done for us, what better motivation do we have than to give him our all, our best? He requires our whole hearts. Do you have the mentality that asks, "How much sin and dirt can I do and still go to heaven?" Many live that very kind of life. If you have that kind of mindset, check where your loyalty lies. Ask yourself, "Am I trying to please my flesh? Or am I trying to please the God that I love?" The right idea is to do everything for God's glory, even when our flesh actively fights for its own way.

There is only one way to deal with the flesh. **Kill it!**

As we seek him, we will serve him. For we "believe that He is and that He is a rewarder of those who seek Him" (Hebrews 11:6). Oh, that our response to sin's call would be as Joseph's response to Potiphar's wife when she invited him to commit adultery with her! In Genesis 39:9 he said, "How then could I do this great evil and sin against God?" That response came out of the love and devotion Joseph had for God. He literally ran away from the enticement of sin. Our love for God and the desire to please him will grow as we draw closer to him.

Reflections

1. Spend a few moments asking God to search your heart for any areas of sin that may be competing for God's spot. Ask God to help you confess and forsake anything that he reveals to you.
2. Do you have gray areas that you indulge in but are not sure whether they are sinful? If so, ask yourself the following: Does doing those things glorify God? Does doing those things enhance your walk with Christ? Could you doing those things cause the

Removing the Dirt in the Church

faith of others to weaken? Does doing those things please your flesh? Do they draw you away from God? Surrender it all to God and respond as you are led.

Prayer

Dear Lord, you deserve all the glory and honor. I do not want to have a divided heart. Please teach me to starve my flesh. Give me the wisdom to enjoy life without sinfully indulging my flesh. Help me to understand how much you love me so that I can love you back without reservation or compromise. Help me to seek you and your kingdom first. In Jesus's name. Amen.

Willful Disobedient

The third attitude we will consider is the willful disobedient. This mindset can occur at all stages of spiritual growth. This is the one who knows what is right and does not do it. They know what is wrong, and yet they do it anyway. They understand the fact that sin has consequences and still choose to walk in it. They have made a conscious decision to do things their own way. In that moment, they don't care about the consequences. They don't think about how it will affect anyone else. They are going to do or not do whatever they have decided. It can happen in a moment, or it can be premeditated. This is the sin of yielding to the flesh. The battle of the Spirit against the flesh will wage until Jesus comes. Giving in to the flesh does great damage to the body of Christ as a whole. Willful disobedience by a Christian is like friendly fire in a war. Your weapons are aimed at the wrong side. But as we yield to and walk in the Spirit, we will grow and not fulfill the lusts of the flesh (Galatians 5:16–25). If we yield to the flesh, we will have to deal with the consequences. In this case, the discipline may be more severe because we know better. If persistent, willful disobedience could possibly forfeit our use for certain ministries and may even cause physical death (1 Corinthians 11:27–32). Many leadership roles

10

The Christian Defined

in the church have qualifications which the persistent willfull disobedient will not meet.

My encouragement to the willful disobedient? Let's grow up, saints! Little babies want to have it their way all the time. Live what you say you believe. If Jesus is Lord of your life, live like it! Life alone brings on enough problems for the Christian. We can afford to do without those problems we bring on ourselves through carelessness, complacency, ignorance, and blatant disobedience. If we suffer, we are blessed if it is for the cause of Christ and not because we are reaping the harvest of seeds sown in disobedience (1 Peter 4:14–16). We have plenty of examples of what not to do. We need more examples of victorious Christians living in this generation who know and believe what the Word says, and who walk in deliberate obedience to it without compromise! Will you be one? God wants to use some plain, ordinary people, young or old, male or female, who dare to put him first. Let's display God's power in us and giving us victory over sin. The world is hungry for the living bread (John 6:35). We need to let him be lifted up in our lives.

> *Willful disobedience by a Christian is like friendly fire in a war. Your weapons are aimed at the wrong side.*

Reflections

1. Spend a few moments asking God to search your heart for areas where you feel sinfully entitled to do things your own way. Think about God's displeasure about your actions.

2. Think about any consequences you have suffered in your past or present from being willfully disobedient. Write down what it cost you. Ask God to heal any hurts and correct all faulty thinking related to willful disobedience in your life.

Removing the Dirt in the Church

Prayer

Thank you dear Father for the times I got caught being willfully disobedient. May they help me to realize that it is never worth it to deliberately displease you. I can choose to sin, but I don't get to choose the consequences that I may suffer. Thank you for loving me enough to discipline me. Thank you for your grace that is greater than all my sin. Please grant me a heart of true repentance. Help me to see sin as you see it and to never knowingly take your grace for granted again. Amen.

Fearful and Unbelieving

When God's character – namely His trustworthiness, power, provision, etc. – is doubted, those who are fearful often decide to take matters into their own hands.

The next mindset we will examine is the fearful and unbelieving. Those in this category have difficulty trusting God and his clearly revealed Word, especially when their feelings or what their senses tell them contradict what God has said. Fearfulness and unbelief often result in disobedience to God's will. When God's character—namely his trustworthiness, power, provision, etc.—is doubted, those who are fearful often decide to take matters into their own hands. Taking action can be a good thing, but not when it is done in opposition to God's clear direction and motivated by fear. Jeroboam's leading Israel in idolatry is an example of this. (See "Unnamed Man of God" in Part 2.) One can have unbelief without fear as well as fear without having unbelief, but they often go together, fueling each other. Despite the fact that God's faithfulness and power to keep his promises has been demonstrated

The Christian Defined

both in God's Word and in the fearful person's life, it seems small in their eyes compared to the what-ifs and the worst-case scenarios swirling in their minds. Past trauma can also lead to fear and unbelief. Sinful people or catastrophic events and the like can cause wounds in us that make it difficult for us to trust anyone, including God.

Another way to view fearfulness and unbelief is a lack of faith in God. God is very patient and gives his people opportunities to grow in faith. He is glorified when his people trust him to act according to his character and his Word regardless of their circumstances. Jesus commended great faith and challenged little faith (Matthew 8:10, 26). God, his character, and his Word, not our wishes, are appropriate objects of our faith. Just because God does not grant our every wish does not mean that he is not trustworthy. Although we live in a fallen world where wicked people do wicked things and devastating tragedies happen, God is still trustworthy. It is especially during these extreme hardships that we need to run to God, not away from him. Failing to trust God is like an assault on his character. The one who is perfectly holy and pure, all knowing, all powerful, and ever present is certainly deserving of our trust. When one has difficulty trusting God, intentional efforts to get to know him more intimately, interpreting past adversities from his perspective, and surrendering to his will may facilitate the growth necessary to trust God even in adverse circumstances. "It is better to take refuge in the Lord than to trust in man" (Psalm 118:8).

> *One can have unbelief without fear as well as fear without having unbelief, but they often go together, fueling each other.*

Reflections

1. How did you learn what you know about God? Is what you believe about God consistent with God's revelation of himself in the Bible? If it differs, how so?

Removing the Dirt in the Church

2. What, if anything, is hindering your trust and reliance on God? What deliberate steps can you take to increase your dependence on God?

3. If you have experienced trauma, have you sought support from a trained counselor? If so, good for you! Continue to do what is necessary to draw near to God. If not, what are your reasons for choosing not to get help? How will you draw near to God for help to remove the barriers of fear and unbelief?

Prayer

Dear Lord, I believe in you. Please help my unbelief. Help me to love you more than my personal comfort. May I intentionally consider what you have already done for me through the sacrificial death and resurrection of Jesus Christ as proof of your love and faithfulness toward me. Let me see you as the almighty, ever-present, and unchanging holy God that you are—bigger than any problem I have ever faced. Help me to depend on the grace that you have provided for me to live a God-dependent life that is well pleasing to you. Please make me better instead of bitter due to sins against me. Teach me to trust, obey, and rest in you. In Christ Jesus's name with thanksgiving, I pray. Amen.

Condescending Prideful

From outward appearances, those in this next mindset may appear to be the epitome of holiness. The condescending prideful are often very disciplined, law-abiding citizens. The problem with this mindset is their prideful attitude. While every disciplined, law-abiding citizen in the church is not a condescending, prideful person, some put confidence in their own works and accomplishments and act as if their works gain them a special standing with God. They fail to acknowledge that it is God who has enabled them to accomplish anything. They often compare themselves

The Christian Defined

to others by putting others down and inflating their own egos. An example of the condescending prideful in Scripture is the Pharisee (Luke 18:9–14).

The condescending prideful wreak havoc in the church because they act as though their opinion is God's opinion. They elevate their preference in nonessential areas to nonnegotiable, often offending their brothers and sisters in the process. God's Word is distorted by their preferences and traditions, which is different than staying true to his Word. This undue focus on nonessentials causes unnecessary division in the church. They act as though they are better than and look down on people who do not agree with them. Instead of seeing disagreement as an opportunity for them to grow or for them to help others grow, they see disagreement as a threat. Winning may become their primary goal instead of representing Christ. When they are in a leadership position in the church, their attitude readily breeds discouragement among laity and causes people to not want to have anything to do with the church. They do not see the sinfulness of their attitude. But God hates this holier-than-thou attitude (Proverbs 6:16–17). We must discern between essentials and nonessentials and in all things humbly communicate with grace and truth. Even when dealing with heresy, a prideful attitude does not glorify God. Those who continue in a condescending, prideful attitude set themselves in opposition to God. "God is opposed to the proud, but gives grace to the humble" (1 Peter 5:5).

> *The condescending prideful wreak havoc in the church because they act as though their opinion is God's opinion.*

Reflections

1. Prayerfully consider your thoughts and responses if you feel irritated when someone questions your authority. Ask God to reveal to you if you have a condescending, prideful attitude.

Removing the Dirt in the Church

2. Do you feel that you are above being questioned? Do you retaliate or seek to lessen someone else's influence if they disagree with you? If yes, ask God to reveal what causes you to retaliate or seek to lessen someone else's influence when they disagree with you.
3. Do you lack patience with others? Ask God to reveal to you if you consider others as less than your equal.

Prayer

Dear heavenly Father, you alone are the most high God. Help me to humble myself before you so that you will not have to humble me. Help me to remember that regardless of what position of authority I may have, that I answer to you. Help me to treat others as valuable people made in your image for whom Christ died and rose again to save. May I be loving, forgiving, gracious, and kind. Help me to ever be a student of your Word who lives what I've learned. May I give you all the glory for every positive thing I accomplish, knowing that any gift and ability I have comes from you. For Christ's sake. Amen.

Counterfeit

The final mindset that misrepresents Christianity is one that comes from the counterfeit Christian. This person is in the church. They may even have a position or title. Outwardly, they may appear to be a "good Christian." Upon closer examination you will find, however, that they are hypocrites and only acting like they are Christians. They don't have a real love for God or his people. When the going gets tough, this counterfeit usually will leave the church because they never made a heart commitment to Christ. Oftentimes, if the culture of the church is not independently strong in the Word, the counterfeit can set up camp and run the church for years. This wolf in sheep's clothing has a territory and will not give it up without a fight. They are very committed, but not to Christ. They may know the Word, but they misapply it. They twist it for their own gain or to cover their sin. They are full of greed

The Christian Defined

and covetousness. A higher value is placed on their rules and on satisfying their flesh than on the needs or growth of the people. Self-recognition is their top priority. Counterfeits can be deceived by the worse kind of deception—self-deception. They keep track of all their "works for the kingdom" with pride. Much like the Pharisees, they think much more highly of themselves than they should. These imposters may think they are doing God a favor, but they don't really know God at all (Matthew 7:21–23). They are actually captives of Satan doing his bidding. But as long as they are alive, there is opportunity for God to grant them repentance so they can come to the knowledge of the truth (2 Timothy 2:24–26).

Counterfeits can be deceived by the worse kind of deception – self-deception.

Reflections

1. Have you ever seen yourself as a sinner in need of rescue by Jesus Christ? If not, ask God to open your eyes to your sin and need for Christ.
2. Is pleasing Christ the motivation for what you do in the church? If not, freshly surrender to his lordship now.
3. Ask God to reveal to you any remaining self-deception you may have.

Prayer

God of heaven, please grant me true repentance from sin and draw me to yourself. Help me to have more than an intellectual knowledge of Christ. Help me to trust in his death, burial, and resurrection for my sins alone for my salvation. I renounce and forsake anything that I previously trusted in. Please forgive me and save me as I call on Jesus's name right now. Thank you, Lord. Amen.

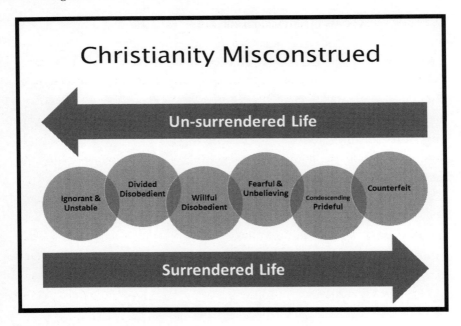

If we are honest, a look into our past may reveal times when we were ignorant and unstable, divided disobedient, or willfully disobedient. We may have had more than one or multiple combinations of these mindsets. Some reading this page may have come to the realization that they do not have a genuine relationship with Christ. The local church is filled with people on the spectrum from ignorant and unstable to counterfeit, as illustrated in the table above. From the outside looking in, a counterfeit may appear to be the most mature in the bunch! This makes the local church sound like a mess! What's the difference between those in and outside of the church? Is the only difference between a Christian and a sinner that one is heaven bound and one is hell bound? As the Apostle Paul would say, "God forbid!" (Romans 6:2 KJV). How can we manage? No wonder so many have decided not to affiliate with a local church body. But there is hope for us all. Leaving the church is not the answer. We are saved by God's grace through faith in Christ's death and resurrection on our behalf. We can depend on him to keep us and empower us to persevere, but we must surrender to him.

The Christian Defined

Surrendered versus Unsurrendered Life

While God supplies the grace that allows us to obey him, it takes purposeful surrender to obey God. Our own flesh and the enemy of our souls can be relentless. Often, those who do not live a surrendered life love to identify with David, a man after God's own heart, who committed adultery and murder (David actually abused his authority in taking Bathsheba—see "My Survivor Story of Clergy Sexual Abuse" in Part Three), and with Abraham, the friend of God, who lied on multiple occasions. They were human, not perfect, so we all can identify with them to some extent. The unsurrendered, however, are practicing a form of self-deception that keeps them from having godly sorrow over their sin. Since they can identify with the friend of God and a man after God's own heart, for them it normalizes their sin as "not so bad." I'm speaking about sin as clearly defined in the Bible and not someone's personal preference or the traditions of men.

The following can be troublesome because here are some examples of language used by both those who truly want to please God and by those who use this language as a cloak to camouflage their sin or take advantage of those who want to please God. To possibly help you identify the latter, consider the following: They love to talk about how undeserving they are, which possibly disguises their sinful hearts as one of humility. They love to talk about unconditional love because they aren't even trying to be lovable. In a moment of "weakness" they mistreat or take advantage of a brother or sister and expect an "I'm sorry" to make things right even though they don't turn from the offense. They keep on offending the person and keep saying "I'm sorry" and expect forgiveness every time. And by forgiveness, they expect that the offended party should act as though nothing ever happened. Notice the inconsistency of what they say and what they do.

Christ told us to forgive our brother, but that does not give one brother free license to do what he wills against his brother. If you have been sinned against, it is not holding a grudge if you wisely make it inconvenient for a person to continue to sin against you. That's wisdom. A surrendered Christian will own their sin, repent (turn from it), and add deliberate action to change and make it right.

Some professing Christians live like sinners and say, "Oh, I'm just a

Removing the Dirt in the Church

carnal Christian. God knows I just won't do right. I won't have any rewards in heaven, but I'm going. I'll see you there." I wouldn't be so sure about that! The person who says that just might be a counterfeit. When I say live like sinners, I'm not referring to the way people dress or even where they go—although wise Christians are careful about how they dress and where they go. I'm referring to the practice of things that are plainly labeled as sin in the Bible. There is no question of whether it's right or wrong. This is a willfully disobedient or counterfeit person. They are doing wrong, and they know they are doing wrong. But they are content just as they are. They aren't trying to grow spiritually. Some may feel bad about their sin, but not bad enough to change. They compare their lives to others instead of to God's standard. Have you ever done that? I have. Ouch. They say, "You're no better than I am, and if you're going to heaven, I know I'm going!" Or they may say, "What can you say to me about my life? Look at yours!" Or this more noble-sounding excuse: "I'm basically a good person. I'm just having a few problems right now." Their "right now" has been months or years, and they still haven't taken deliberate action to change. They love to be around people who don't practice holiness, and as for people who do practice holiness, "they're being self-righteous" or "they can't relate" because they are out of touch since they (the ones who live righteously) may not have experienced the struggles that they (who are carnal) have. They have to show the "wrong" in those who are living righteously in order to ease their own conscience. This "carnal Christian" may even attempt to trap the righteous in sin so that their holy lifestyle will not convict them.

That behavior is not living by faith. It's a waste of time. Even demons believe that there is one God, but are they pleasing to God (James 2:19)? No, because it takes more than just intellectual belief. It takes belief in action. Faith without works is not saving faith. "Faith without works is dead" (James 2:26). If all you have is faith without works, you are spiritually dead. So we see that we do have a responsibility to act according to our faith. How do we do that? The answer is really simple. We must believe, surrender, and obey God's Word. God's Spirit indwells the believer and supplies the power needed to obey. The Word is full of instruction. We have Jesus as our example. We are to learn from, obey, and imitate him. And yes, he does expect obedience. It is only through obedience to him that we show our love for him (John 14:15).

The Christian Defined

No man can serve two masters. Whomever we serve is our master (Romans 6:16). We are to measure our actions and lifestyle against his Word and by his grace make every effort to obey. It's basically a matter of choice. We must choose his will over our will; his will over the will of any other; his will over the world's trends. It really is a matter of choice, heart, soul, mind, and might, on our part. Of course, we need God's help to do right and please him. If we could please God on our own, we wouldn't need salvation, would we? Works alone are insufficient to save and keep us because we can't work well enough to meet God's standard (Isaiah 64:6). It takes a heart of faith in Christ to the point of action (confession and repentance) to save us, and that salvation is evidenced by faith in Christ to the point of action (obedience).

God has given every person the capacity to be saved. We were created in his image with a mind. We can think and choose. To every Christian, God has given the capacity to obey. His Word and his indwelling Holy Spirit have already been freely given to us. The Lord has prepared the table for us. We must simply eat the food! Our food does not jump from the plate to our stomachs. We must lift the food to our mouths, chew, and swallow it first! Then we will benefit from its nourishment and grow. God's Word does not leap from the pages into our lives. We must open his Word and take the time to "study to show [ourselves] approved unto God" (2 Timothy 2:15 KJV) and "meditate [in it] day and night" (Psalm 1:2 KJV). His Spirit does not take over our faculties. We must yield them to him as stated in Romans 6:16. We must take deliberate steps to get closer to him. Regularly read and study the Bible. Regularly attend a Bible-believing, Christ-centered church. We must regularly fellowship with other believers. Those are just a few beginning steps. As we get closer to God, he gets closer to us. It's a supernatural growth that happens within. But we are responsible to respond to God's call. He calls us to salvation and to holiness. He's waiting to do his supernatural work in us, but we must do our part. God doesn't want robots. He could have created us to do only what he programmed us to do, but he wants us to choose. Christians can practice holiness! We are exhorted to build on our faith. To our faith, we are to add virtue, and to virtue knowledge, and to knowledge temperance, and to temperance patience, and to patience godliness, and to godliness brotherly kindness, and to brotherly kindness charity (love). If we would

21

Removing the Dirt in the Church

diligently make our calling and election sure by practicing these things, we wouldn't fall or practice ungodliness (2 Peter 1:3–10).

To practice sin and know it is foolishness. It is like a man building a house on sand. In the storm it will be utterly destroyed and so will the one who knowingly practices sin without effort of correction (Matthew 7:26–27). Practice means just that—doing something over and over repeatedly. Practice means a way of life. Sometimes we practice things we aren't aware of, and before long it's a habit. It usually works out that it's easy to make bad habits but hard to break them. That is why we must deliberately practice righteousness. If we don't, you can bet we're practicing unrighteousness. If we do not take time to learn about our new Master and the power he has given to us over sin, we will forget that we have been purged from our old sins (2 Peter 1:9). We naturally do that which is familiar to us. We were born in sin, and that's what we're familiar with. We can change with God's help if we practice.

> *If you have the mentality to premeditate sin, you really don't have the right picture of what salvation is all about.*

David, a man after God's own heart, abused his authority, but abuse of authority was not a way of life for him. Yes, he tried to cover his sin with murder, but murder was not a way of life for him. David repented. He turned away from his sin and dealt with the consequences of his sin. We must all deal with the consequences of our sin. The Bible is full of men who weren't perfect. It is also full of the consequences of their sin and folly. So, to those who look at David and say, "I can do it once and still be a Christian," I say count the cost! It's just not worth it. The Word commands us to "make no provision for the flesh" (Romans 13:14). Ephesians 5:3 tells us that "immorality or any impurity or greed must not even be named among [us]." If you have the mentality to premeditate sin, you really don't have the right picture of what salvation is all about.

The Christian Defined

Self-Examination Time

Test and see if you have saving faith. Satan wants to deceive you into hell. If he can make you think you are saved when you are not, you will be in for a rude awakening. Counterfeits before the throne of God will declare what they did in his name. Christ will declare to them that "I never knew you" (Matthew 7:21–23)! Satan seeks to destroy you completely. When the Word says that "all liars shall have their part in the lake which burns with fire," it means all (Revelation 21:8 NKJV). There are no exceptions. When it says that no "fornicators, nor idolaters, nor adulterers ... will inherit the kingdom of God" (1 Corinthians 6:9–10), it means just that. To be Christian and a liar is inconsistent. To be Christian and adulterer or fornicator is inconsistent. John says, if you think you are both, you are deceived (1 John 2:4). Why live bound to sin when Christ can set you free? If you continue in your charade, you will have to deal with serious consequences. Eternal separation from God in the lake of fire for eternity!

How can we grow to be mature Christians that God can use to build his kingdom? How can we avoid getting caught in the same vacuum of sin over and over again? How can we deal with wolves in our churches? We need to get to know the Answer for ourselves. No matter which category or mindset someone is in, the solution to their sin problem is the same: repentance and trust in the finished work of Jesus Christ. There is hope for all truly repentant people as there is no sin that the blood of Jesus cannot cleanse. As we appropriate that cleansing and grow to maturity, God will use us to show others the Way. He will also use us to hold others accountable and to contend for the faith (Jude 3). We are at war! When Christians do not deal with sin in their lives, they give an opportunity for the way of Christ to be maligned and to possibly be a stumbling block to others who would come to Christ (Romans 2:24). Much to their own peril, they are joined with Satan to war against their own souls. Let's see what we can glean from the downfalls of biblical characters so that we will not be ignorant of Satan's devices.

Part 2

Down and Dirty

Biblical Characters

The Israelites were God's chosen people. He did not choose them because of any inherent greatness on their part (Deuteronomy 7:6–8). They were just people. People like you and me. In Down and Dirty, we will see some missteps of individuals among God's beloved people to help us examine ourselves and aid in our avoiding the same. In addition to individual's sins, we will expose sin on a systemic level both in Israel and in today's church.

Aaron

Aaron, Moses's older brother, was one of the leaders of the children of Israel. God comforted Moses's feelings of insecurity at his initial call by telling him that his brother Aaron would go with him and be a mouthpiece for him. Aaron served as a liaison between Moses and the people, and he accompanied Moses when he went before the pharaoh. Aaron got a front-row seat to all the displays of God's power through the ten plagues, the great deliverance of the children of Israel crossing the Red Sea on dry ground, and the pharaoh's army drowning when they followed them onto the dry seabed. Aaron's witness of God's power over nature and the enemies of Israel did not inoculate him from the pressure of disgruntled people.

Moses taught the people God's commandments and explained

Removing the Dirt in the Church

his covenant, which the people agreed to follow (Exodus 24:3). After formalizing this covenant between God and the people, Moses went on the mountaintop and left the people in the care of Aaron and Hur. Moses was gone for forty days and forty nights (Exodus 24:13–18). And although the Israelites saw the glory of God, which looked like fire on top of the mountain, they told Aaron to make them a god who would lead them because they didn't know what happened to Moses. The Bible doesn't say anything about Aaron trying to dissuade them from that idea. Instead, he complied with their request, instructing them to bring gold rings from the ears of the people, which he made into a molten calf. Aaron even made an altar for it and proclaimed a feast for the next day. The people worshiped and sacrificed to a metal calf, breaking the first two commands that God had given them (Exodus 32:1–6).

> I am the Lord your God, who brought you out of the land of Egypt, out of the house of slavery. You shall have no other gods before Me. You shall not make for yourself an idol, or any likeness of what is in heaven above or on the earth beneath or in the water under the earth. You shall not worship them or serve them; for I, the Lord your God, am a jealous God, visiting the iniquity of the fathers on the children, on the third and the fourth generations of those who hate Me, but showing lovingkindness to thousands, to those who love Me and keep My commandments. (Exodus 20:2–6)

The people had agreed to do all that the Lord had spoken, yet when Moses delayed, the first thing they did was break covenant with God by worshiping a golden image. God saw their idolatry and told Moses that he would pour out his wrath upon them, wipe them out, and start over with Moses, making a great nation from his offspring instead. Moses interceded for the people in defense of God's reputation among the nations. He didn't want the Egyptians to think that God delivered his people with evil intent only to destroy them (Exodus 32:11–14).

Moses left the people in Aaron's care, but Aaron failed to point the people back to God. He let the people's impatience pressure him to comply

26

Down and Dirty

with their request even though he knew better. Aaron had been with the elders as they beheld the form of God and ate the covenant meal (Exodus 24:9–11). He knew that what he had previously seen was no metal calf that he could form with his own hands. Aaron complied with the people, but at what cost? About three thousand people died from the sword of judgment from the Lord through the sons of Levi (Exodus 32:25–28). In addition to that, the Lord sent a plague upon the people because they worshiped the calf that Aaron made (Exodus 32:35).

Aaron aided the people in straying from the Lord. As an excuse, he later told Moses how the people were so prone to wander; yet he had helped them in their wandering. The Bible does not give us insight into the motives behind Aaron's actions. Perhaps he was afraid of the great multitude of people. Maybe Aaron also became impatient and wondered what was taking Moses so long. Did he see this situation as an opportunity for him to gain favor among the people? Whatever his motivation, it was

Are you a people pleaser?

unacceptable to God for him to make the golden calf and declare a feast to it and condone the worship of it. You may say, "I'll never worship a statue!" But idolatry has many facets. Placing anything or anyone above God and his will is idolatry (1 Samuel 15:23—Saul's rejection as king). Some church leaders today may cave to pressure from the people to speak the type of messages they want to hear or to conduct activities in the church that do not glorify God. Are you a people pleaser? Do you hold fast to God's Word through your leadership (Titus 1:7–9)? Will you be judged for leading others astray (Matthew 18:7)? Know this: "The fear of man brings a snare" (Proverbs 29:25). What will you hear when you stand before God? Will you hear "well done"? You can! Live and lead so that you can say like Paul, "Be imitators of me, just as I also am of Christ" (1 Corinthians 11:1).

Removing the Dirt in the Church

Reflections

1. Think about areas in your life where you have leadership responsibility. Are you a people pleaser? Ask God to reveal your heart. How would you lead to please God better?
2. If the people under your leadership were to follow you, would they live in obedience to God? Ask God to change you, if necessary.
3. How do you develop vision and goals as a leader? Ask God to help you acknowledge him in all your ways.

Prayer

Dear heavenly Father, I can't lead myself, let alone your people, without your help. Please guard my heart against self-reliance and straying from you through people pleasing. Help me to lean and depend on you as the one who sees, knows, and can do all things. May my public and private life be reflective of my complete trust and dependence on you. Help me to follow everywhere you lead and teach others to do the same. In Jesus's name. Amen.

Miriam

Miriam, the sister of Moses, is introduced in the Bible as such—Moses's sister (Exodus 2:4). Moses was God's chosen deliverer to lead his people from bondage in Egypt to the promised land. This section is about Miriam; however, her story is closely connected to Moses's story. When Moses was born, his mother hid him for three months. When she could no longer hide him, she constructed a small waterproof basket, placed him inside, and put it among the reeds by the bank of the Nile. Miriam, his sister, stood at a distance to see what would happen to him. When the pharaoh's daughter came to bathe in the Nile, she saw the basket. After sending her maid to retrieve it, she opened it, saw the baby crying, and had pity on him as she recognized him as one of the Hebrew children. Miriam

Down and Dirty

spoke up and asked the pharaoh's daughter if she would like her to find a nurse from among the Hebrew women to nurse the child for her. She told her to do so, and Miriam went and called the baby's mother. The pharaoh's daughter actually paid this woman to nurse her own baby (Exodus 2:1–10)!

This was, of course, part of God's sovereign will as he would one day use this baby to lead his people in the exodus from Egypt. Until he grew old enough to go live with the pharaoh's daughter, Moses lived in his birth home as part of the family with his parents and older siblings: Miriam, his sister, and Aaron, his brother.

Miriam, as a Hebrew, learned about Jehovah God. She saw that her brother was spared the tragic fate of other boy babies born in Moses's time. Even amidst the bondage of her people, many years later, she had hope that things could change because her brother, who was raised as the son of the pharaoh's daughter, was like a prince in Egypt. Perhaps he could influence them to release the Hebrews from slavery. But Miriam would have to be patient. It would be about eighty years before God revealed to Moses his plan to use him to deliver the Israelites.

The pharaoh did not cheerfully let the people go. Moses went back and forth before him several times with God's message, "Let My people go!" And each time the pharaoh hardened his heart. God sent plague after plague, demonstrating his mighty power over all objects of Egyptian worship; but it wasn't until after the tenth plague, the death of the firstborn of both man and cattle, that the pharaoh finally let the people go (Exodus 7–11; 12:29–32). For more about how God miraculously delivered the Israelites, see the section on Moses or Exodus 14.

God's people were free at last! They sang to the Lord, extoling his great deliverance. Miriam, now well above eighty years old, took a timbrel, and all the women followed after her with timbrels and dancing. Miriam is referred to as a prophetess in this account (Exodus 15:20–21). Although the specifics of her role(s) are not clearly delineated, she was sent by God as one of the leaders of the people alongside Moses and Aaron (Micah 6:4). Perhaps she saw her role as one of equality with Moses.

One day both she and her brother Aaron spoke against Moses because he had married a Cushite woman (Numbers 12). They questioned, "Has the LORD indeed spoken only through Moses? Has He not spoken through us as well?" (Numbers 12:2). On the surface, this may seem like

29

a harmless question, but it was not. The Lord heard it and called the three siblings to the meeting tent. God's presence came down to the doorway of the tent. He rebuked Aaron and Miriam, citing his unique mode of communication directly with Moses, mouth to mouth, rather than in visions or dreams as he did with other prophets, and allowing Moses to behold his form. On this basis, God questions them: "Why then were you not afraid to speak against My servant, against Moses?" (Numbers 12:8). Their actions angered God, and when the cloud lifted, Miriam was leprous! When Aaron saw that she was leprous, he begged Moses to intercede for her. Moses immediately prayed that she be healed, but God said that she must be shut up outside the camp for seven days (Numbers 12:1–15).

The Bible does not say why Miriam was the only one who experienced leprosy. It may be that she instigated this situation. But God knows the heart, and his judgments are just and right (Jeremiah 17:10). God is God. He does not answer to us about the objects of his favor. He does what he pleases (Psalm 115:3). Whatever problem Miriam had with Moses marrying the Cushite woman, it did not give her the right to bring into question whom God chose to speak through.

Personal preference is never to cause division among the body of Christ.

This example does not mean that we can't question when anyone is in blatant sin. If someone sins, we are to go to them in a spirit of meekness (Galatians 6:1). Meekness, however, is not what Miriam displayed. Since the Bible does not speak of any sin on Moses's part, anything addressing such would be speculation. What is clear from this text is God's displeasure with Miriam. He was so displeased that Scripture warned the next generation of the children of Israel not to forget what God did to her (Deuteronomy 24:9). Since this was written for our learning, we also would be wise not to forget it (Romans 15:4).

Oftentimes people in the church can be jealous of a fellow Christian's position or influence in the church. When this

Down and Dirty

motivates them to speak negatively about others or to actively work to lessen or destroy the influence of others, God is displeased. One who does this causes unnecessary division, allowing themselves to be a tool of the enemy. Personal preference is never to cause division among the body of Christ. Moreover, one who does this may experience God's judgment as a result. If you think you could do a better job than someone else, or if you think someone shouldn't be in the position that they are in, take it to God in prayer. It's his business. He uses whom he chooses. Remember, "pride goes before destruction, And a haughty spirit before stumbling" (Proverbs 16:18).

Reflections

1. What, if any, strong opinions about non-sin issues do you have regarding what others should or shouldn't be doing in their lives? What concern is it of yours?
2. What gift(s) and calling(s) are you aware that God has given to you? If you are unaware of them, ask God to show them to you. Spend time giving God glory for the gifts he has given you and others.
3. Are you able to appreciate the gifts and callings of others without feeling insecure in your own gifts? If not, ask God to help you see him at work in others.

Prayer

Heavenly Father, you are the giver of gifts. All good things come from you. Thank you for choosing to give leadership gifts to the body of Christ to be used for your glory. Give me discernment to see if I am envious of your choice to use others in your kingdom work. Help me understand that your use of others does not limit your use of me. May I glorify you as you work through your people. May I also yield to you as you prepare me to be fit for your use. Have your way in me, Lord. In your name I pray. Amen.

31

Removing the Dirt in the Church

Ten Spies

God faithfully kept his covenant promise to Abraham and multiplied his descendants. He delivered them from bondage as promised (Genesis 15:5–14). God provided for their every need, including bread from heaven to eat each day as they wandered in the wilderness on the way to the promised land of Canaan. Their destination was described by God as a land flowing with milk and honey (Exodus 3:8). Under Moses's leadership, the children of Israel journeyed in anticipation of reaching a land of abundance where they could dwell securely as God's prized possession. When they finally reached the promised land, Moses sent twelve spies, one representing each of the twelve tribes of Israel, to scout out the land (Numbers 13:1–21).

The spies went into the land and spent forty days observing the cities, people, and fruit of the land. They brought a sample of the fruit from the land to show to the Israelites. It was so luscious that a single cluster of grapes had to be put on a pole and carried by two men (Numbers 13:22–26).

When the spies shared the report with Moses and the Israelites, they verified that it was indeed a land flowing with milk and honey. Caleb, the spy representing the tribe of Judah, affirmed that they should go up and take possession of the land. He believed that they would be victorious. But there was one problem. Ten of the spies were intimidated by the people of the land. They failed to believe that God would give them the victory as he had done in their previous battle with Amalek at Rephidim. The unbelieving spies told Moses and the people that the people of the land "are stronger than we are" (Numbers 13:31 NIV) and "are of great size" (Numbers 13:32 NIV). They expressed that they (the spies) were "like grasshoppers in our own eyes" (Numbers 13:33 NIV) compared to the men of the land (Numbers 13:27–33).

When the people heard the negative report of the ten spies, they grumbled against Moses and Aaron and accused the Lord of bringing them into the land only for them to die in battle. Then to make matters worse, they suggested picking a new leader to lead them back to Egypt! Caleb and Joshua, in an effort to keep the people from rebelling against God, tried to reason with them that with God on their side, there was no

Down and Dirty

reason to fear the people of the land. But the people refused to listen and wanted to stone Caleb and Joshua (Numbers 14:1–10).

Moses and Aaron fell on their faces before God in response to the people grumbling against them and God. The unbelief of the ten spies spread like gangrene throughout the Israelite camp and resulted in the people rebelling against God. Once again, God expressed to Moses his intention to destroy the nation of grumbling unbelievers and start over with Moses's descendants. Moses interceded on behalf of the people citing God's reputation among the nations. They would think that God slaughtered them in the wilderness because he could not keep his promise to bring them into the land. God decided instead to allow the next generation of Israelites to go into the land, but the unbelieving generation, who were twenty years old and upward, would die in the wilderness as they wandered for forty years. The ten unbelieving spies died by a plague before the Lord. Of all the spies, only Caleb and Joshua lived and entered the promised land (Numbers 14:11–38).

Many in the church today want every decision in the church to be made by a majority vote. That is not necessarily a bad thing, especially for major decisions. This narrative, however, illustrates a clear case in which the majority was wrong. These twelve spies were leaders in their tribes entrusted to gather helpful intel about the land they were about to possess. They all saw the same thing, but ten of the twelve seemed to forget both that God had promised them the land and his faithfulness to meet their every need up to this point. When fear and failure to trust God is motivating the majority, it can wreak havoc in the church.

When fear and failure to trust God is motivating the majority, it can wreak havoc in the church.

In addition to fear and unbelief, personal preference can cause immature people to be prideful. This is why it's so important not to have immature people in positions of leadership in the church (1 Timothy 3:6). They may use their influence to stir up negativity

33

Removing the Dirt in the Church

in the church because upper leadership does not do things according to their inclinations. The Bible speaks against divisiveness for divisiveness's sake (Romans 16:17; Titus 3:10). By all means, speak up if senior leadership is straying from sound doctrine and wisdom. Choose your battles carefully. But be warned that if you have impure motives or are merely expressing your personal preferences, you may find yourself on the wrong side of the battle for which there will be consequences from God himself.

Reflections

1. How does the majority opinion influence your decision making? How can you ensure that seeking God's guidance is first place in your decision-making process? Ask God to help you to desire and seek his guidance first.
2. What tends to motivate your opinions most? Do they tend to be motivated more by fear than by what God says? Do you know and understand for yourself what God says? Ask God to help you know and trust what he says for yourself.
3. How willing are you to humbly stand against the majority when they are opposed to God's clear will as written in his Word? What has courage looked like when you must stand alone? Ask God to increase your courage to stand biblically for him.

Prayer

Dear Father, you are bigger than any problem or giant that I have or ever will face. Help me to trust that you will keep your word to your people. Help me to know and trust you and what your Word says for myself. Give me courage to always stand with you even if I must stand alone, because I know that I am never truly alone. You are always with me. Help me live like I know this. Amen.

Down and Dirty

Korah and Company

Being a leader can be unceasingly draining. In Numbers 16, the continuing saga of the Hebrews as they journeyed to the promised land, Moses faced yet another confrontation. Korah, Dathan, and Abiram, along with 250 other leaders of the congregation, stood against Moses and challenged his authority. Their complaint was that Moses and Aaron exalted themselves over the people. They argued that each person in the congregation was holy and that the Lord was among them just as he was with Moses. They served Moses notice that he had gone far enough.

Moses's classic response was to fall on his face before God, which he did. Moses then proposed a showdown for God to confirm who indeed was his choice. The next day, they were to each bring a censer with incense before the Lord. Moses let them know that they were the ones who went too far. He reasoned with them about how God had chosen them for special service related to the tabernacle and to minister to the people, but they weren't satisfied with that. They wanted the priesthood too.

When Moses summoned Dathan and Abiram to come up, they refused and accused him of bringing them out of a land flowing with milk and honey only to have them die in the wilderness. They actually referred to Egypt, where they had been slaves, with the descriptor that God used for the land of promise. They seemed to forget that they would have been in the promised land already had they believed God instead of the evil report from the ten unbelieving spies. They continued saying that Moses had not kept his end of the bargain. They weren't brought to a land flowing with milk and honey, nor were they given an inheritance. They accused Moses of duping them.

Moses was angry and prayed that God would not accept their offering. When they all assembled before the Lord the next day, the Lord spoke to Moses and Aaron and told them to separate from the congregation so he could destroy them all. Moses and Aaron fell on their faces and interceded for the people so that God would not be angry with the entire congregation on account of one man. God then commanded Moses to speak to the congregation and command them to move away from the tents of Korah, Dathan, and Abiram.

Removing the Dirt in the Church

> Then Moses arose and went to Dathan and Abiram, with
> the elders of Israel following him, and he spoke to the
> congregation, saying, "Depart now from the tents of these
> wicked men, and touch nothing that belongs to them,
> or you will be swept away in all their sin." So they got
> back from around the dwellings of Korah, Dathan and
> Abiram; and Dathan and Abiram came out and stood
> at the doorway of their tents, along with their wives and
> their sons and their little ones. Moses said, "By this you
> shall know that the Lord has sent me to do all these
> deeds; for this is not my doing. If these men die the death
> of all men or if they suffer the fate of all men, then the
> Lord has not sent me. But if the Lord brings about an
> entirely new thing and the ground opens its mouth and
> swallows them up with all that is theirs, and they descend
> alive into Sheol, then you will understand that these men
> have spurned the Lord." As he finished speaking all these
> words, the ground that was under them split open; and
> the earth opened its mouth and swallowed them up, and
> their households, and all the men who belonged to Korah
> with their possessions. So they and all that belonged to
> them went down alive to Sheol; and the earth closed over
> them, and they perished from the midst of the assembly.
> (Numbers 16:25–33)

In addition to Korah, Dathan, and Abiram getting swallowed up alive, their families also died because of their rebellion. Fire from God consumed the 250 men who were offering incense before the Lord. God made it very clear who his choice was. Korah and company were not rebelling against Moses and Aaron. They rebelled against God. Their judgment was not from Moses but from God.

The next day, the people grumbled against Moses and Aaron and blamed them for the death of "the Lord's people," Korah and company. God told Moses to get away from those murmuring people so that he could destroy them. Moses once again interceded for the people, but there were consequences. The Lord sent a plague, and 14,700 people died.

Down and Dirty

To further illustrate that Moses and Aaron were God's choice to lead the people, God had each tribe to submit a rod on which the family name was inscribed. Aaron's name was on the rod for the tribe of Levi. They were put before the Lord in the Tent of the Testimony. The following day, Aaron's rod "had sprouted and put forth buds and produced blossoms, and it bore ripe almonds" (Numbers 17:8). God instructed Moses to place the rod that budded back before the testimony as a sign to would-be rebels (Numbers 17:1–11).

It's interesting how Korah's premise that the entire congregation was holy was valid (Deuteronomy 7:6). Unfortunately, he came to a wrong conclusion that because they were holy, Moses and Aaron could not have authority over them. Korah thought that because Moses operated in the office given to him by God that he was lording it over the people. Despite Korah's poor reasoning, he and his entourage were able to influence 250 others. That could have been intimidating to Moses, but he knew who he was. God's testimony about Moses was that he was the meekest man of all the people on the face of the earth (Numbers 12:3). Korah's accusation against Moses was false, but that did not stop him and others from trying to take over.

There are people in the church today who, instead of working with church leadership, incite rebellion against it. The reasons are varied, but often not valid. When this happens due to reasons other than unrepentant sin within the leadership, they, like Korah, are really rebelling against God. Rebellion against God does not persist without consequences (1 Samuel 12:15). While God may not open the earth and swallow you whole with your family and all your possessions, know that God will have the last word. There may come a time to stand up against authority. Learn to discern, or else you may find yourself fighting against God, to whom we must all give an account (Romans 14:12).

Rebellion against God does not persist without consequences.

37

Removing the Dirt in the Church

Reflections

1. How do you utilize the influence that you have as a person? What effect, if any, does your influence have on other people's walks with God?
2. Think about yourself as a follower. How do you discern whether or when to question or follow a leader?
3. Have you ever experienced consequences in your life or seen someone else experiencing consequences after working against a biblical, God-fearing leader? A non-biblical leader? Ask God to teach you to discern for yourself who truly represents him.

Prayer

Father God, thank you for placing order among your people. Just as there is order yet equality within the Godhead, help us understand that it is your will to have order with equality in the church. Would you please teach us to discern what that means and how to carry it out? Teach us to function within our God-given roles, realizing that we are all representing and serving you. Help us to function in biblical unity. In Jesus's name. Amen.

Moses

Moses is known in the Bible as the man God used to deliver the Israelites from slavery in Egypt and to give his law. For those unfamiliar with Moses's story, here's some abbreviated context from the book of Exodus. God's people, the Hebrews, were so numerous that the pharaoh viewed them as mightier than the Egyptians. He devised a plan to deal shrewdly with the Hebrews because he feared they would side with the Egyptians' enemies in the event of war. First, he afflicted them with hard labor; that did not slow their population growth. Then he commanded the Hebrew midwives to put the Hebrew baby boys to death and only allow the baby girls to live. That also did not work because the midwives feared

Down and Dirty

God and allowed the boys to live. Finally, the pharaoh commanded all his people that every Hebrew baby son was to be cast into the Nile (Exodus 1:8–22).

> By faith Moses, when he was born, was hidden for three months by his parents, because they saw he was a beautiful child; and they were not afraid of the king's edict. (Hebrews 11:23)

When his mother could no longer hide him, she put him in a basket that she had waterproofed with tar and pitch and placed him among the reeds along the bank of the Nile. God in his sovereignty allowed this baby to be found and adopted by the pharaoh's daughter and nursed by his birth mother (Exodus 2:1–10). Until he grew old enough to go live with the pharaoh's daughter, Moses lived in his birth home as part of the family with his parents and older siblings, Miriam and Aaron. We imagine his mother taught him his true heritage because the Bible testifies that Moses later refused to be called the son of the pharaoh's daughter and chose to suffer with the people of God rather than enjoy the passing pleasures of sin (Hebrews 11:24–26).

Moses attempted to deliver his brethren when he was forty years old. It resulted in him having to flee for his life because he killed an Egyptian who was mistreating a slave. He thought no one saw him as he buried the dead man in the sand. The next day, however, he found that someone did see, and the pharaoh now wanted to kill him. So he fled to Midian (Exodus 2:11–15).

Many years later, after the death of the king of Egypt, God, speaking through a burning bush, miraculously disclosed to Moses his plan to free his people from enslavement. Although he was initially hesitant, Moses finally answered God's call to go and deliver God's message to the pharaoh to let his people go (Exodus 3, 4). If you've read this in the Bible or seen the classic movie *The Ten Commandments*, you know the pharaoh's heart was hardened. Instead of letting the people go, he intensified their labor. But God demonstrated his mighty power through ten plagues. The pharaoh would promise to let the people go to gain relief from the current plague, but as soon as he had respite from the plague, he would renege on his

Removing the Dirt in the Church

promise to let the people go. Then God would send another plague. God made a distinction between where the Egyptians lived and where the Hebrews lived so that all would know that the God of the Hebrews is the sovereign God. After the last plague, the death of the firstborn of man and beast, the pharaoh finally let the people go (Exodus 7–11; 12:29–32).

The pharaoh, however, changed his mind again, gathered his army with horses and chariots, and pursued his former slaves. The people feared and complained to Moses when they saw the Egyptian army coming after them. They thought they were trapped, but God intervened. His presence in a pillar of cloud kept the Egyptians away from Moses and the Hebrews. God commanded Moses to lift his hand over the Red Sea. It miraculously parted and formed a path that allowed the people to cross on dry ground. When the cloud between them lifted, the Egyptians gave chase, only to find that God was fighting against them (Exodus 14:9–25). The chariot wheels began to swerve, and they had difficulty driving. At God's command, Moses stretched his hand over the sea once more and the sea returned to its place, drowning the Egyptians, the chariots, and their horsemen (Exodus 14:26–27).

> The waters returned and covered the chariots and the horsemen, even Pharaoh's entire army that had gone into the sea after them; not even one of them remained. But the sons of Israel walked on dry land through the midst of the sea, and the waters were like a wall to them on their right hand and on their left. Thus the Lord saved Israel that day from the hand of the Egyptians, and Israel saw the Egyptians dead on the seashore. When Israel saw the great power which the Lord had used against the Egyptians, the people feared the Lord, and they believed in the Lord and in His servant Moses. (Exodus 14:28–31)

God's mighty rescue of his people was finally over. Moses and the people could not help but sing praises to the Lord (Exodus 15:1–21). They were filled with awe and amazement after witnessing God's power displayed on their behalf. It would be great if the narrative continued with "and they went straight to the promised land and lived there happily ever

Down and Dirty

after." But that is far from what happened. Although the people were free from the Egyptians, they were in the wilderness. They wandered there for forty years because of Israel's unbelief. They faced challenges, such as a lack of water, and God miraculously provided whatever they needed. In hindsight, toward the end of their journey, Moses explained to the Israelites why God allowed them to face multiple problems in the desert.

> You shall remember all the way which the Lord your God
> has led you in the wilderness these forty years, that He
> might humble you, testing you, to know what was in your
> heart, whether you would keep His commandments or
> not. (Deuteronomy 8:2)

While they were being tested, Moses was right there leading them, teaching them, interceding for them, and giving them God's messages and judgments. Leading that great multitude of people for forty years was an arduous task, to say the least. Yet the Bible says that Moses was very humble, more than any man on the face of the earth (Numbers 12:3). And despite God's track record of always supplying their needs, often miraculously, the children of Israel had a pattern of murmuring and complaining when things didn't go their way.

On one occasion again the congregation of Israel was in a challenging situation (Numbers 20:1–13). They were in the wilderness with no water to drink. Instead of believing that God would miraculously provide what they needed as he had numerous times before, they accused Moses of bringing them into the wilderness to die. Moses and Aaron fell on their faces before the Lord.

> Take the rod; and you and your brother Aaron assemble
> the congregation and speak to the rock before their eyes,
> that it may yield its water. You shall thus bring forth water
> for them out of the rock and let the congregation and their
> beasts drink. (Numbers 20:8)

Moses got the rod as commanded and gathered the people before the rock. But on this occasion, Moses's indignation with the people's complaining got the best of him. Instead of speaking to the rock as commanded by God, Moses called the people rebels and struck the rock twice (Numbers 20:9–11). Now, it's quite understandable that Moses was frustrated with the people. He had been listening to their whining for forty years. But Moses had also reverenced God by obeying him in all that he had commanded him.

This time, however, Moses did not follow God's command exactly. In another situation when they didn't have water (Exodus 17:1–6), God had commanded Moses to strike a rock and plenty of water came out for the people and the animals to drink. Here God's command was for Moses to speak to the rock. Although Moses struck the rock twice, God still graciously provided the water. But Moses would have consequences for his failure to comply with God's explicit directions.

> *Just as Moses's years of faithful service did not give him a free pass to disobey God without repercussion, we cannot and will not earn one either.*

But the Lord said to Moses and Aaron, "Because you have not believed Me, to treat Me as holy in the sight of the sons of Israel, therefore you shall not bring this assembly into the land which I have given them." (Numbers 20:12)

Moses had been faithful throughout his leadership of the children of Israel up to this point, humbly leading, teaching, judging, and interceding for the people. His misstep near the brink of the promised land is a poignant warning for all leaders and Christians. God said that Moses did not believe him and treat him as holy before the people. Here's the lesson. Just as Moses's years of faithful service did not give him a free pass to disobey God without repercussion, we cannot and will not earn one either. Do not allow years of walking with God to lull you into laxity. No matter the trials or challenges we face, God is always worthy of our full trust and obedience. Everyone

Down and Dirty

will answer for their actions before God. Disobedience has consequences. Be faithful to the end (James 1:12) and finish well (1 Corinthians 9:24)!

Reflections

1. In what ways might you have become lax and presume that he is pleased with you? What areas in your life will you ask God to help you intentionally seek to obey him to the end?
2. Are you burned out? Seek God to restore and energize you by his grace.
3. At times when you lack patience during challenging circumstances or with immature people, what Scriptures do you need to implement most? Ask God to help you obey him no matter how immature the people are or how challenging the circumstances you face are.

Prayer

Father, it is sobering to know that Moses did not make it into the promised land. Help me to remember, if I am in a leadership position, that when the people complain when I am following and obeying you, they are really complaining against you. Help me not to take it personally. Help me to remember that I am serving you through serving your people. Please help me to stay humble, learn from Moses, and finish well. Amen.

Achan

The story of Achan is found in chapter seven of the book of Joshua. He was a soldier under Joshua's leadership in the army of the children of Israel. After wandering in the wilderness for forty years, they finally arrived at the promised land. Joshua and the people of God miraculously crossed the Jordan River on dry land (Joshua 3:7–17). Their first battle to possess the land was against the city of Jericho. Joshua received unique battle

Removing the Dirt in the Church

plan instructions from the Lord. Joshua followed them exactly, and they overwhelmingly conquered Jericho (Joshua 6).

The next city was much smaller. But after their first attempt to conquer the small city of Ai, they had to retreat in defeat. Joshua cried out to the Lord only to find that someone in the camp failed to follow the instruction of the Lord about the loot from the previous battle. God had instructed the people that Jericho and everything in it was under a ban. The silver, gold, bronze, and iron were holy and belonged to the Lord. Everything else was to be utterly destroyed. He warned them before the battle that coveting and taking things under the ban would make the camp of Israel accursed and bring trouble on it. And trouble is what they got. God told Joshua that they would not be able to stand before their enemies, and that he would not be with them anymore unless they destroyed the things under the ban from within the camp (Joshua 7:1–12). What an indictment!

God instructed Joshua to have the people come before his presence the next morning by tribes. God would single out the guilty tribe from within the twelve tribes. He would single out the family from within the group of families that made up the guilty tribe. He would single out the household from within those households that made up the guilty family. Finally, he would have them come, man by man, from the guilty household to make known to Joshua and the people who had sinned by taking the forbidden things for himself. Achan was selected (Joshua 7:13–18).

> Then Joshua said to Achan, "My son, I implore you, give glory to the LORD, the God of Israel, and give praise to Him; and tell me now what you have done. Do not hide it from me." (Joshua 7:19)

Only after having the camp go through that entire process did Achan confess what he had done. He saw, coveted, took, and then hid a cloak, some silver, and a bar of gold inside his tent. Joshua sent messengers who discovered the things, just as Achan had confessed. They brought the items and poured them out before the Lord (Joshua 7:20–23).

Then Joshua and all Israel with him, took Achan the son of Zerah, the silver, the mantle, the bar of gold, his sons, his daughters, his oxen, his donkeys, his sheep, his tent and all that belonged to him; and they brought

Down and Dirty

them up to the valley of Achor. Joshua said, "Why have you troubled us? The LORD will trouble you this day." And all Israel stoned them with stones; and they burned them with fire after they had stoned them with stones. They raised over him a great heap of stones that stands to this day, and the LORD turned from the fierceness of His anger. Therefore, the name of that place has been called the valley of Achor to this day. (Joshua 7:24–26)

Achan's sin did not affect him alone. The Israelites who died in the battle at Ai, the families of those who died, and Achan's sons, daughters, livestock, his tent, and everything that belonged to him was destroyed. I'm sure that were Achan alive today to speak for himself, he'd say that it was not worth it to disobey God. Achan could not claim that he didn't know that what he did was wrong. He hid the things because he knew he wasn't supposed to have them. Achan's sin with its consequences serve to remind us today that God is to be obeyed. Don't rationalize yourself into sin because you don't believe anyone will find out. Even if God does not deliver instant consequences for disobedience, please know that God sees all. Be sure your sin will find you out (Numbers 32:23). If you have stolen, lied, or cheated, make it right while you have time. He's giving grace, which if received will lead to repentance (Romans 2:4). Repent and receive God's amazing grace today!

> *Were Achan alive today to speak for himself, he'd say that it was not worth it to disobey God.*

Reflections

1. Are there things that you lie about or hide because you know they're wrong, and you do not want to get caught? If so, repent and make them right so far as humanly possible.

Removing the Dirt in the Church

2. Do you try to get ahead by doing unbiblical or illegal things if you feel you can do it and not get caught? Ask God to help you to trust his provision and timing to walk in obedience to his will.

3. If God were to show you any areas of compromise where you may take inappropriate shortcuts, do the wrong thing for a noble reason or the right thing in an unbiblical way, what would the specifics be? Ask God to help you walk in wisdom and holiness.

Prayer

Gracious heavenly Father, you are so holy! Help me to understand as much as humanly possible how impeccably holy you are. May your holiness influence my every decision. Please keep me from greed, dishonesty, self-will, and self-deception. Help me to walk in holiness as you are holy. Give me the desire and strength to please you more than I want to please myself and to trust you to supply my needs. In Jesus's name. Amen.

Unnamed Man of God

There is an unnamed man of God in 1 Kings 13 who came out of Judah. As the narrative goes, this man of God obediently went to Bethel to deliver the word of the Lord against the altar that King Jeroboam had built in rebellion to the God of Israel. The temple of the Lord was in Jerusalem, and God's people were commanded to offer sacrifices and celebrate various festivals there. The kingdom of Israel had just been divided, and Jeroboam was king over ten tribes of Israel. Solomon's son, Rehoboam, was king over Judah and Benjamin.

Motivated by the fear of losing his life and his newly acquired kingdom, Jeroboam decided that it would be best if the people under his rule did not go to the temple of the Lord at Jerusalem to offer sacrifices any longer. King Jeroboam mandated two sites for worship—complete with a golden calf at each as the object of worship—and appointed priests to administrate the worship. These priests were not of the tribe of Levi whom God had

Down and Dirty

ordained under Moses. Jeroboam led the people into idolatry although God promised him an enduring kingdom if he would do right in God's sight (1 Kings 11:38). How sad that Jeroboam was fearful and unbelieving.

By the word of the Lord, the man of God proclaimed that a future king from David's lineage by the name of Josiah would desecrate this altar with the human bones of the false priests who used the altar for idolatry. God also had given a sign on the same day that authenticated the man of God's message—the altar would be torn down and the ashes poured out—which happened just as the man of God proclaimed.

Now this man of God started off well. He had obediently proclaimed God's message even though it was not a welcome one. He saw God's protection of him when King Jeroboam's hand dried up as he stretched it out to give the command for the man of God to be arrested. The king stretched out his hand but could not draw it back. It was restored only after the man of God prayed for him. If the man of God had any doubts that he had heard from the Lord, the sign of the altar being torn down that came to pass, God drying the king's hand, and God restoring the king's hand was surely sufficient to banish them.

After the king's hand was restored, he graciously invited the man of God to come to his home, be refreshed, and receive a reward. The man of God declined the king's offer, citing a command from God that he "eat no bread, nor drink water, nor return by the way [that he] came" (1 Kings 13:9). Then he proceeded to obey God's command by leaving another way.

The message that the man of God delivered was definitely a pronouncement of judgment. There was an old prophet there at Bethel who went after the man of God and tricked him into coming home with him for a meal. This old prophet had heard from his sons the details of the exchange between the man of God and King Jeroboam. He went and found the man of God and invited him back to his home in Bethel for a meal. The man of God initially declined citing the command he had received from God not to eat bread or drink water in that place. But upon hearing the old prophet affirm that he, too, was a prophet and that an angel spoke to him by the word of the Lord commanding him to bring the man of God back to his house so he could eat bread and drink water, he accepted the old prophet's invitation. Unfortunately for the man of God, the old prophet lied, and he was deceived into disobeying God's command

Removing the Dirt in the Church

not to eat nor drink there. The old prophet from Bethel then pronounced a word from the Lord that because the man of God had disobeyed the command that the Lord his God gave him, "Eat no bread and drink no water," his body would not come to the tomb of his fathers. What a disastrous turn of events for the man of God from Judah!

Many times, in the narrative of Scripture, we are given details such as motives and conditions of the heart of Biblical characters. This is not the case, however, in this particular Bible story, so we cannot be sure why the man of God from Judah believed the old prophet from Bethel. Perhaps he was hungry, and food and fellowship sounded good to him. Camaraderie among fellow prophets was probably a rare and welcomed opportunity. Or maybe he just naively believed the old prophet because he was older and professed to be a prophet too. No matter the reason, we can learn from his unfortunate fate. Just as the old prophet lied for his own benefit (so his bones would not be defiled on the altar as prophesied), there are those who lie today for their own benefit. The Bible is replete with warnings about false representatives who claim to be speaking for and serving God. Christians cannot afford to naively believe everyone who says that they have a word from the Lord. Study Paul's reprimand to the Galatian churches for straying from the true gospel:

> *Christians cannot afford to naively believe everyone who says that they have a word from the Lord.*

But even if we, or an angel from heaven, should preach to you a gospel contrary to what we have preached to you, he is to be accursed! As we have said before, so I say again now, if any man is preaching to you a gospel contrary to what you received, he is to be accursed! (Galatians 1:8–9)

Paul repeated for emphasis that regardless of the source, we are not to entertain another gospel. While the prophet in this Old Testament narrative was not preaching the gospel of salvation, he was preaching the

48

Down and Dirty

confirmed word of God. We have the Word of God, the Bible, and we need to pay attention to it (2 Peter 1:19–21)! We must learn to obey God rather than men regardless of their authority or title (Acts 5:29).

Reflections

1. Think about how you process information you receive from those who represent God. Do you consider it in light of what you have studied for yourself? Do you automatically assume that it is the rightly divided Word of God? Do you allow their personal opinions to become your personal opinions without thinking for yourself? Ask God to teach you and help you to use biblically based spiritual discernment.

2. When God is leading you to do or not to do something, how are you able to discern his will? How well are you able to tell the difference between your wishes and God's? Ask God to help you to delight in him so that his desires and yours will be the same.

3. After reaching adulthood, have you ever automatically assumed that the assertions of those older than you are always right? Ask God to help you learn the art of humbly and respectfully disagreeing when necessary.

Prayer

Dear heavenly Father, thank you for recording this incident in the narrative of Scripture. Help me to learn from it and use biblical discernment regardless of appearances knowing that Satan disguises himself as an angel of light. Please remove any hint of naivety from my heart and mind. Help me to know your voice and to confidently follow you without fear. Thank you for the assurance that your Word will never fail. May I walk in the light of your Word all of my remaining days. I pray in the matchless name of Jesus. Amen.

Removing the Dirt in the Church

Pharisee

If you've ever thought of Jesus as someone so gentle that he would never say a harsh word, think again. A quick survey of Jesus's conversations with Pharisees in the New Testament would demonstrate otherwise. Jesus could see into the hearts of men, and many Pharisees had wicked hearts. In Matthew 23, Jesus warned the multitude and his disciples not to do as the scribes and Pharisees do because "they say, and do not" (Matthew 23:3 KJV) [i.e., they didn't practice what they preached]. "Whoever exalts himself shall be humbled; and whoever humbles himself shall be exalted" (Matthew 23:12).

Beginning at Matthew 23:13 and through verse 33, Jesus chided the scribes and Pharisees several times, calling them hypocrites, fools, and blind while citing examples of their sinful actions that supported his judgment. The root of those sinful actions was pride. "But woe to you, scribes and Pharisees, hypocrites ..." The word "but" contrasts the prideful scribes and Pharisees with whoever humbles himself in the previous verse. The scribes and Pharisees presented themselves as the experts who spoke for and represented God. But they did not accurately represent God. They were prideful hypocrites. "God is opposed to the proud, but gives grace to the humble" (James 4:6). No wonder Jesus clashed with the Pharisees so often!

Pride also affected the Pharisees' view of others. Examine this parable from Luke 18 in which Jesus denounced pride and to whom it was directed.

> And He also told this parable to some people who trusted in themselves that they were righteous, and viewed others with contempt: "Two men went up into the temple to pray, one a Pharisee and the other a tax collector. The Pharisee stood and was praying this to himself: 'God, I thank You that I am not like other people: swindlers, unjust, adulterers, or even like this tax collector. I fast twice a week; I pay tithes of all that I get.' But the tax collector, standing some distance away, was even unwilling to lift up his eyes to heaven, but was beating his breast, saying, 'God, be merciful to me, the sinner!' I tell you, this

man went to his house justified rather than the other; for everyone who exalts himself will be humbled, but he who humbles himself will be exalted. (Luke 18:9–14)

The Pharisee in this parable mistakenly thought that his "good works" made him better than others who did not do all that he did. He trusted in himself that he was righteous because of his deeds. He failed to acknowledge God, who enabled him to do the things he did. God gave him the health and strength to fast twice a week. God gave him the substance from which he could tithe. He saw himself as unlike other people, when in reality, "all [people] have sinned and fall short of the glory of God" (Romans 3:23), including him! No one can earn God's favor through their own efforts. Salvation is by grace through faith in what Christ has done on our behalf (Titus 3:4–7).

So deceived was this Pharisee that he, exalting himself, thanked God that he was not "even like this tax collector." He was right, but not like he thought. He was not like the tax collector because the tax collector was aware of his sinfulness and humbly asked God for mercy. The Pharisee's pride canceled out his "good works," and God opposed him. He did not leave the temple justified, but the tax collector, in his humility, did.

Don't play the comparison game or you may deceive yourself into thinking you are better than other people. You are not. All people are made in God's image, but we have been marred. None of us are better than others because we are all in the same sinful condition (Romans 5:12). If you want to compare yourself to someone, compare yourself to Jesus, the sinless one. Then you will see how far from the mark you fall! Don't trust in yourself that you are righteous. Your own righteousness is like a filthy garment (Isaiah 64:6). The word filthy is from the Hebrew word *iddâ* which means menstruation (Harris 1980, 645). That is how unclean our own righteousness is before God—like a filthy menstrual garment! Do you want God to oppose you? Or do you want his grace freely

> *If you want to compare yourself to someone, compare yourself to Jesus, the sinless One.*

Removing the Dirt in the Church

given to you? His grace is unlimited. Humble yourself before him; receive his grace (James 4:6); let him exalt you (James 4:10).

Reflections

1. Think about the good works that you do. Do you feel that what you do entitles you to the favor of God? Do you believe that they make you more valuable to God than others who don't do what you do? What would Jesus say of you if you were the example in his object lesson?
2. How would God grade you on the humility scale? Ask God to help you to stay humble before him so that he will not have to resist you.
3. On what do you place your confidence to stand before God? Reflect on the truths that we are accepted by God and enabled to do good works for God's glory only because of the righteousness of Christ.

Prayer

Father, please fix my heart. Forgive me for prideful attitudes and for comparing myself with others even if only in my heart. Remove any remaining self-reliance. Help me to be truly pleasing in your sight inside and out. Thank you for enabling me to do good works for your glory. Thank you for Jesus's example of humility. Help me to cooperate with the process as you conform me to his image. Thank you in Jesus's name. Amen.

Peter

Peter was a passionate follower of Christ. As one of Jesus's inner circle within the twelve apostles, he was often very opinionated and freely spoke his mind. So bold was Peter that on one occasion, Peter took Jesus, the one whom he had proclaimed to be the Christ, the Son of the living God, aside and rebuked him after he foretold the apostles of his future suffering, death, and resurrection on the third day (Matthew 16:15–23). On another occasion, after the Passover meal, Jesus explained to the apostles that they would all be scattered as a result of his arrest that very night. Peter boldly answered that even if everyone else fell away he would never fall away, but Jesus told Peter that he would deny him three times that very night before the cock crowed. Peter then expressed that he would die before he denied Jesus (Matthew 26:31–35).

Peter did indeed deny the Lord three times before the rooster crowed, but in his heart of hearts, prior to it happening, he did not believe he was capable of doing such a thing. There is often a gap between where we are in our hearts and where we think we are. Peter was out of touch with the condition of his heart. He did what he said he would never do. This is not uncommon, as it is easy to confuse in our minds where we are with where we desire to be. We often do not see our own biases about ourselves, because we think we know better than anyone what our intentions are. Jeremiah asserts that "the heart is more deceitful than all else" (Jeremiah 17:9). We often can't understand our own hearts. But while that may be true of people, it is not true of God. He is the only one who perfectly knows our hearts.

A fall can be a blessing if it causes us to look up to God and rely upon Him.

It can be pretty devastating to find that we are nowhere near where we thought we were. Just as Peter wept bitterly after denying Jesus three times, we may weep after having done what we said we'd never do, after the cover has been pulled back and another facet of our wretched hearts has been exposed. But just as there was hope for Peter, there is hope for us. Just as Jesus had prayed for Peter, Jesus has prayed for us (John 17:20). Whatever we did that was shockingly contrary to where we thought we were was not a shock to God. If we have a difficult time getting over our own sin and failures, this may indicate that we have a pride issue.

After a devastating failure, some may be tempted to try to make up for it by trying harder to be perfect from now on. This is not the answer,

Removing the Dirt in the Church

as it is based on self-reliance and performance. If we could be perfect by trying harder, we wouldn't need Jesus, would we? We are to be faithful depending upon God's enablement, not our own. In fact, God can use our failures to increase our humility and reliance upon him. Humility is an important virtue in the Christian life because God is to get all of the glory for what is accomplished in and through us. God actually resists the proud but gives grace to the humble (1 Peter 5:5–6). It is God's grace that saves us and keeps us. We are warned in 1 Corinthians 10:12 that if we think we are standing, to take heed lest we fall. No matter what we have done, cleansing from our sin and self-reliance can be found in the blood of Jesus. A fall can be a blessing if it causes us to look up to God and rely upon him. As we depend upon him, we can walk in the good works that God has ordained us to accomplish.

Peter's denial of Christ was not the end of the story for him. He went on to boldly proclaim the gospel on the day of Pentecost and continued to boldly preach, even facing jail as a consequence. He was used by God to provide leadership in the early church and to pen sacred Scripture and was eventually martyred for his faith. His finish was a far cry from the scaredy-cat who denied Jesus. If you failed in a way that you thought you never would, do not let your failure define you. There is hope. Like Peter, by God's grace, you can rise above your failings and be used by God again.

Reflections

1. Have you as a follower of Christ done something displeasing to God that you thought you would never do? If so, thank God for the lessons you are (were) able to learn from that experience.

2. Have your past sins hindered you from moving forward despite your having repented for them? How might God redeem and use those past failures for his glory?

3. If you were to resolve to share your testimony with others, what parts would you share? Ask God to help you to share whatever he leads you to share for his glory.

Down and Dirty

Prayer

Dear Lord God Almighty, I don't want to fail you. I want to hear you say to me, "Well done, good and faithful servant." You are not surprised by anything that I do. Help me to understand that and to fully surrender to your redeeming work in my life. Please show me my sin and the weaknesses that I need to surrender to you. Thank you for the assurance that when I repent and turn from my sin that you will immediately cleanse and forgive me. Thank you for your grace, which helps me to grow through every consequence I may need to experience. Help me to trust that you can still use me for your glory. I surrender to you now. In the name of Jesus Christ, I pray. Amen.

Saul/Paul

Saul of Tarsus, before his encounter with Christ on the road to Damascus, was very zealous for God, or so he thought. One of God's chosen people, he was raised to know and obey the laws of God. He was also a Pharisee, which meant that he was a religious leader. The religious leaders of Jesus's day did not recognize him as the Messiah and viewed this new sect of Jesus followers as a threat to Judaism. Saul instigated the persecution of the early Christians and sought approval from the high priest to find and bind Christians who had scattered to Damascus and return them to Jerusalem. It was on the road to Damascus that he was blinded by a light from heaven; he was confronted by Jesus and became a follower of Christ. Though temporarily blind, he could finally see Jesus as the Messiah. He was called to be an apostle to the Gentiles, and gladly preached the risen Christ and suffered for his name. Saul later became known as Paul (Acts 13:9).

Before his conversion, Paul believed a lie. He thought he was doing the right thing by persecuting the Christians. He had a great zeal for God, but it was not according to knowledge of the Christ as prophesied in the Scriptures that he claimed to believe. Jesus was indeed the promised Messiah, but Paul believed the Christians were wrong for following Jesus.

55

Removing the Dirt in the Church

Have you ever believed a lie? Or thought you were right and found you were wrong? It can be easy to do when everyone else in your group is thinking the same wrong way. It's especially easy when the leaders or experts in the group are thinking that way. Sometimes, we follow the belief system of our parents or other leaders in our lives without question. However, it behooves us to examine the claims of Christ for ourselves. Jesus made some pretty bold statements that demand a response on our part for which we will be held accountable. We do not have to stay ignorant. If with a sincere heart we ask God to show us his truth and seek for it, we will find it.

> *We do not have to stay ignorant.*

This is Paul's personal testimony as shared in 1 Timothy 1:12–16:

> I thank Christ Jesus our Lord, who has strengthened me, because He considered me faithful, putting me into service, even though I was formerly a blasphemer and a persecutor and a violent aggressor. Yet I was shown mercy because I acted ignorantly in unbelief; and the grace of our Lord was more than abundant, with the faith and love which are found in Christ Jesus. It is a trustworthy statement, deserving full acceptance, that Christ Jesus came into the world to save sinners, among whom I am foremost of all. Yet for this reason I found mercy, so that in me as the foremost, Jesus Christ might demonstrate His perfect patience as an example for those who would believe in Him for eternal life.

The acceptance of truth in the apostle Paul's life produced a change that was both immediate and dramatic. The people in Damascus were shocked to learn that the man who once zealously sought to persecute Christians now preached Christ. Eventually the Jews there plotted to kill him, but this did not discourage Paul. He continued to boldly proclaim the gospel wherever he had opportunity and wherever the Spirit of God

Down and Dirty

led him. God subsequently used him to write at least thirteen books of the New Testament. Paul's life demonstrates that the lies we believed in the past do not of necessity limit God's use of us in the present or future. Before Paul's conversion, he was sincere, but he was sincerely wrong about Christ. After his conversion, he was sincere and set free by the truth of the gospel of Christ. He was free to worship and serve Christ, boldly sharing him unashamedly with as much or more zeal than he had as a persecutor of the church. Scripture asserts that God had chosen Paul to bear his name before the Gentiles and kings and the children of Israel (Acts 9:10–20). Paul was the perfect person to preach and write about the riches of God's grace.

If you thought you were right in rejecting Christ and perhaps taught others to do the same, or if you have found that you were wrong about some other spiritual truth, there is mercy for you just as there was for Paul. If you have committed what you consider to be the worst of sins, know for certain that Christ's sacrificial death, burial, and resurrection is sufficient to save you too. Confess, surrender, and believe God now, and he will enable you to walk in the truth. Humility is key. If you see yourself as an "expert," it may be difficult for you to see your own error, but it's not difficult for God to enlighten you. Admitting to others your previous misunderstanding and giving the correct truth(s) may be in order especially if you previously propagated mistruths. It is a testament to God's grace that he chooses to show us our faulty thinking. As we continue to study his Word, the Bible, he will continue to illuminate our minds to what is true and enable us to apply it to our lives.

Reflections

1. Have you ever believed a lie as an adult? If so, how did it affect your life? How did you come to know the truth?
2. What changes can you make to become a better student of God's Word?
3. Spend time thanking God for the truth of his Word.

Removing the Dirt in the Church

Prayer

Father God, thank you for the encouraging hope that I receive from the conversion of Saul. You are the same God today as the God that I read about in your Word. Just as you got Saul's attention and got him on the right course, I can trust you to take what I feel is the worst that I could have done and put me on and keep me on the right course. Correct all my misunderstandings. Please help me to rightly divide and live according to your Word. Don't let me lead anyone astray. Help me to zealously follow you and live in the freedom that Christ paid with his blood for me to have. Use me however you see fit. In Jesus's precious and holy name, I pray. Amen.

Systemic Sin in Israel and the Church

We have seen instances of sin in the lives of individuals. We will now look at sin from a systemic perspective. In the Old Testament and in Jesus's day, Israel was supposed to be a theocracy—under God's rule. The leaders were charged with leading the people as God directed them through his prophets, priests, and eventually, kings. In this section, we will see that was not always the case. The leaders misrepresented God, and the people mistreated one another.

Shepherds of Israel

In Ezekiel 34, God commanded the prophet Ezekiel to prophesy against the shepherds of Israel. Shepherds in this passage can refer to both kings and priests of Israel. The kings and priests were to be supported by the people (sheep). But they were in turn to be cared for by the leadership. God was not pleased with the shepherds because they were only feeding themselves to the neglect of feeding the flock. This was nothing short of abuse. Let's look at what God says through his prophet, Ezekiel:

Down and Dirty

Then the word of the Lord came to me saying, "Son of man, prophesy against the shepherds of Israel. Prophesy and say to those shepherds, 'Thus says the Lord God, "Woe, shepherds of Israel who have been feeding themselves! Should not the shepherds feed the flock? You eat the fat and clothe yourselves with the wool, you slaughter the fat sheep without feeding the flock. Those who are sickly you have not strengthened, the diseased you have not healed, the broken you have not bound up, the scattered you have not brought back, nor have you sought for the lost; but with force and with severity you have dominated them. They were scattered for lack of a shepherd, and they became food for every beast of the field and were scattered. My flock wandered through all the mountains and on every high hill; My flock was scattered over all the surface of the earth, and there was no one to search or seek for them.""" Therefore, you shepherds, hear the word of the Lord: "As I live," declares the Lord God, "surely because My flock has become a prey, My flock has even become food for all the beasts of the field for lack of a shepherd, and My shepherds did not search for My flock, but rather the shepherds fed themselves and did not feed My flock; therefore, you shepherds, hear the word of the Lord: 'Thus says the Lord God, "Behold, I am against the shepherds, and I will demand My sheep from them and make them cease from feeding sheep. So the shepherds will not feed themselves anymore, but I will deliver My flock from their mouth, so that they will not be food for them.""" (Ezekiel 34:1–10)

God expected the leaders to feed the flock, strengthen the sickly, heal the diseased, bind the broken, bring back the scattered, and seek for the lost. This was not done, and as a result, the sheep were scattered and became prey. God declared that he was against his shepherds because of their gross neglect of the sheep and the resultant vulnerable condition they

59

Removing the Dirt in the Church

suffered. God affirmed that he himself would deliver his flock from the shepherd's mouths.

Eli, Hophni, and Phinehas

An Old Testament example of specific shepherds who displeased God were the priest Eli and his sons, Hophni and Phinehas, also priests. They lived after the time of the exodus from Egypt and entering the promised land, but before the time of the kings. This period is known as the time of the judges. Unfortunately, during those times, people did what was right in their own eyes. They repeated a cycle in which they strayed from God. God allowed them to be oppressed by their enemies, they would cry out to God for help, and God would deliver them through various judges. Often, the people would follow God as long as a particular judge was alive. But after the judge died, they would go back to doing their own thing (Judges 2:10–19).

As priests, Eli and his sons were supposed to know and teach the people all that God required. The people of Israel who wanted to please God relied on the priests. According to the law as given through Moses, one of the major duties of the priests included assisting the people with their prescribed offerings to God. Although priests did not have their own land to cultivate, they were sustained through their duties as priests. They received specific portions of what was offered to God by the people as commanded by God through the law.

Priests were generally well cared for, but the sons of Eli, in disobedience to God, not only wanted more than their authorized share of meat from the sacrifice offered to God, but they also took it (1 Samuel 2:12–16). Before the fat, which belonged to God, was burned off, they would take the meat (Leviticus 3:16). In addition to mishandling God's offerings, they slept with the women who served at the doorway to the Tent of Meeting, which was God's sanctuary (1 Samuel 2:22). Their father, Eli, knew what they were doing. He verbally rebuked them for their sins, but he failed to restrain them. By failing to stop them, he was allowing them to continue their violations against God and his people. God was displeased with Eli and his sons.

> Then a man of God came to Eli and said to him, "Thus says the Lord, 'Did I not indeed reveal Myself to the house

Down and Dirty

of your father when they were in Egypt in bondage to Pharaoh's house? Did I not choose them from all the tribes of Israel to be My priests, to go up to My altar, to burn incense, to carry an ephod before Me; and did I not give to the house of your father all the fire offerings of the sons of Israel? Why do you kick at My sacrifice and at My offering which I have commanded in My dwelling, and honor your sons above Me, by making yourselves fat with the choicest of every offering of My people Israel?' Therefore the Lord God of Israel declares, 'I did indeed say that your house and the house of your father should walk before Me forever'; but now the Lord declares, 'Far be it from Me—for those who honor Me I will honor, and those who despise Me will be lightly esteemed. (1 Samuel 2:27–30)

God rebuked Eli for honoring his sons above God. Eli's responsibility to God was more important than any loyalty to his sons. They broke God's command by eating the part intended for God and defiled women instead of helping in their purification. Eli did nothing but ineffectively talk and probably ate the forbidden part of the sacrifice as well. "Yourselves" in verse 29 included Eli. This was a systemic problem because the priests were ordained by God to help the people walk in holiness. They could not function as intended by God because they themselves were practicing sin. God expected Eli to do more than just talk to correct his sons for disobeying God. Honoring God means to treat him with the respect and obedience that he deserves as God. His commands are not optional suggestions. As part of God's judgment against the house of Eli, the man of

Receive any delay in judgment as the patience of God giving you an opportunity to change your ungodly behavior and make things right.

Removing the Dirt in the Church

God also told Eli that Hophni and Phinehas would both die on the same day (1 Samuel 2:34). And it happened just as he said. In fact, Eli, Hophni, and Phinehas all died on the same day (1 Samuel 4).

Unfortunately, in the church today, people are sometimes honored above God. From the pulpit to the pew, sin is not appropriately handled. It does not matter if someone is in a leadership position, is wealthy, is related by blood to leadership, is highly educated, or famous. God expects all people in the church to do things his way. Whether, as in the case of Hophni and Phinehas, it is an attitude of covetousness or more overt sin such as stealing, all sin is to be seriously dealt with—not just talked about. God may not cause those guilty of honoring others above him to all die on the same day, but he will hold them accountable (Hebrews 10:30). Receive any delay in judgment as the patience of God giving you an opportunity to change your ungodly behavior and make things right. There is no respect of persons with God (Colossians 3:25). And "it is a fearful thing to fall into the hands of the living God" (Hebrews 10:31 KJV).

Sheep of Israel

In addition to his judgment against the shepherds in Ezekiel 34, God also stated that he would also judge between the sheep. He said he would destroy the fat and the strong sheep because as they fed in good pasture, they tread down with their feet the rest of the pastures, making it difficult for others to feed. As they drank clear waters, they fouled the water with their feet so that others could not also drink clear water. They pushed the weak aside with their horns until they were scattered. Listen to what God says to his sheep:

> "As for you, My flock, thus says the Lord God, 'Behold, I will judge between one sheep and another, between the rams and the male goats. Is it too slight a thing for you that you should feed in the good pasture, that you must tread down with your feet the rest of your pastures? Or that you should drink of the clear waters, that you must foul the rest with your feet? As for My flock, they must eat what you tread down with your feet and drink what you

Down and Dirty

foul with your feet!'" Therefore, thus says the Lord God to them, "Behold, I, even I, will judge between the fat sheep and the lean sheep. Because you push with side and with shoulder, and thrust at all the weak with your horns until you have scattered them abroad, therefore, I will deliver My flock, and they will no longer be a prey; and I will judge between one sheep and another. (Ezekiel 34:17–22)

It is no surprise that, in an environment where leadership takes evil advantage of the people charged to their care, others within the group would take an every-man-for-himself attitude. God expected the sheep to be considerate of one another. To make room for each other and consider how their individual actions may affect other sheep. These sheep failed to love their neighbor as themselves (Leviticus 19:18). God declared that he would feed these inconsiderate sheep with judgment, and he would deliver his flock.

God made it clear that he would make things right. He would not only deliver his flock, but he would shepherd, protect, and provide for his sheep (Ezekiel 34:22–24). God went on to describe how wonderful things will be under his rulership. God's rulership is coming. It would be advantageous for us to ensure that we are on the favorable side of his judgment! Let's examine sin in the church system, see how it differs, and what God expects of His people in the church age.

Sin in the Church System

Jesus was very displeased with the religious leaders of his day. He criticized the Pharisees and Sadducees because they were hypocrites. The religious leaders were supposed to facilitate the peoples' relationship with God, but instead they exploited it. Jesus warned his disciples of the scribes who puffed themselves up, devoured widows' houses, and prayed long prayers for appearance's sake (Luke 20:46–47). Instead of being a blessing to the widows, they took advantage of them. Jesus pointed out a widow who gave in the treasury of the synagogue all that she had to live on, contrasting her with those who gave from their abundance. He did not commend this action of the widow. He was contrasting the motives of the

63

Removing the Dirt in the Church

scribes with the motives of the widow. In Luke 11:39, Jesus's indictment of the Pharisees was that they were full of greed and wickedness. The writer of Luke also highlights that the Pharisees were lovers of money (Luke 16:14).

As then, there are religious leaders today who for what the Bible calls "filthy lucre" are devouring widows' houses and fleecing the flock (i.e., taking unfair advantage under false pretense) of the people of God in the name of God. Some individual churches and religious broadcasters alike are guilty of manipulating people into giving more than they can afford to give. They often do this by declaring that it is God's will that the people give a certain amount. In addition, they promise that God will grant a special blessing to those who have faith enough to give what is asked. Many popular leaders claim to have a supernatural "anointing" (more powerful than what average Christians have) and promise that God will grant a specific increase to those who "sow into" the "anointed" person's ministry. Some people may reason that "if the man/woman of God says it is God's will that everyone give a specified amount of money, then I need to obey because I want to demonstrate to God that I have faith. I may be already behind on my bills and other financial obligations, but God will really bless me if I give this." This attitude does not please God, as the Bible exhorts believers to render unto Caesar the things that are Caesar's (Mark 12:13–17; Romans 13:6–7). When you take Caesar's money and give it to the church's building fund, this does not please God. Unfortunately, in many cases, the ministries they supported are nowhere to be found when these people lose their homes or crumble under the mountain of debt that they have accumulated. The naive Christians' witness is tarnished, and they may become spiritually disillusioned as a result of being exploited.

Financial irresponsibility of individual churches and ministries is another culprit that can unnecessarily financially burden its supporters. This can occur when the pastor or leadership implements a vision for the church that does not match the financial intake of the current membership. The vision may not be sinful in and of itself, but the implementation of it through manipulation or impure motives is sinful. If having the biggest and shiniest building, leaving a legacy in the name of the founding or current pastor, or doing what all the other well-known churches are doing is the goal, then perhaps reexamination of the motives is in order. Who's really getting the glory? If the answer is not God, then again, it's time for

64

Down and Dirty

a heart check. Some pastors may be unaware of the undue influence that their position of authority can have on their parishioners; however, they are still accountable to God for how they use that influence. If they are communicating that a particular thing is God's will when it is only their personal desire, that communication is a misrepresentation of God for which they will have to answer to God.

Religious leaders today may also allow how the offering plate may be affected by various situations to shape leadership decisions instead of God's will as clearly written in the Bible. For example, there is a failure to deal with sin among the laity because the leaders fear the sinning member's anger and possible subsequent failure to continue financially supporting the church. Likewise, there is also the problem of failing to biblically respond to sin among leaders themselves for fear of a decrease in donations among the people. Sins of leadership are often minimized or covered up in an effort to keep financial support steady. Unfortunately, even crimes committed by leadership have been covered up in an attempt to keep things "in-house."

Sexual sin among church leadership is another major problem that runs rampant in the church today. The abuse of power to engage in exploitative sex victimizes children and adults alike. This problem spans denominational, cultural, and socioeconomic lines (Short 2004). While it is well-known that any type of sex between adult clergy and a minor is both unlawful and unethical, it is a less known fact that the same is true in many states of sex between clergy and an adult parishioner (Pooler 2017). Just as clergy can misuse their influence for financial gain, they can also misuse it for sexual gratification. In fact, in the Roman Catholic Church, clergy sexual misconduct among adult victims is thought to be more widespread than among child victims (de Weger 2016). It is unfortunate, however, that in adult cases, most often the victim is blamed (Morey 1988). This should not be the case as there is an unequal distribution of power between clergy and parishioner.

Oftentimes, parishioners believe that they can trust what their clergy says as being from God. When they have doubts, many will second-guess themselves before doubting the clergy, because clergy are supposed to be God's spokespeople. While clergy in most denominations are considered merely human, it is not unrealistic to expect them to speak as God's

Removing the Dirt in the Church

representative because that is what they are. It is a reasonable expectation that congregants should be able to go to their clergy for godly counsel without being exploited in their time of vulnerability. Therefore, true consent cannot be given in these cases. It is nothing less than spiritual and sexual abuse.

> *It is often at the time of a congregant's greatest need, that wayward clergy will use their gift of influence to use and abuse parishioners to satisfy their own lusts.*

In many cases of clergy sexual abuse with both children and adults, there is a grooming process during which the Scriptures are twisted to coerce the victim to become dependent upon the clergy for wisdom, to yield to sexual advances by the clergy, and to afterward keep their secret (Garland 2006). This misusing of the Scriptures can be especially confusing to those who are committed to obey God's Word despite personal cost as commended in Scriptures. In fact, those who are wholly devoted to God are often victimized. Some congregants do not have confidence in their own ability to hear from God, especially during a time of, or in the aftermath of, a crisis. In their desire to sincerely seek God, they go to their clergy for professional spiritual guidance (Garland 2006). The clergy merely must convince them that it is "God's will" for them to do or not do something. It is often at the time of a congregant's greatest need that wayward clergy will use their gift of influence to use and abuse parishioners to satisfy their own lusts.

In addition to covering up sexual sins against parishioners, churches have been guilty of covering up when leadership is guilty of crimes against their own family members, such as in cases of incest or domestic violence. The Scripture that forbids fellow Christians from going to court to settle a disagreement is used out of context to convince the victims not to expose

66

Down and Dirty

the person who is committing these crimes against them (1 Corinthians 6:1–7). Paul rebuked the Corinthians for going to court over disputes without even trying to resolve it among the saints. Mature saints should be able to mediate disputes biblically. Disagreements between church members and the crimes of incest and domestic violence, however, are two different things. Paul commanded that the church remove from fellowship the person who was having sex with his father's wife because immorality should not be tolerated in the church (1 Corinthians 5). Incest and domestic violence are no less immoral. Paul states in Romans 13 that rulers are God's ministers for good. They administer wrath on God's behalf on the one who practices evil. The person committing incest and domestic violence are doing evil. Those who do evil should be afraid. Failing to expose them only emboldens them to continue sinning because they are assured that no one will do anything about it. Why not pressure the person doing wrong to turn themselves in instead of pressuring the person who has been sinned against to keep things quiet? In any case, discounting these crimes and not doing anything about them is not a biblical option. At the very least, providing support and comfort for those in need is in order. Blaming the person being sinned against is definitely not what Jesus would do. Christians are instructed to obey the laws of the land. Domestic violence and incest are both against the law. The person committing such sins should be considered a sinner until their actions show a change of heart. Repentance has fruit.

On the other side of the spectrum from failing to deal with sin at all is the overzealous, holier-than-thou attitude that is quick to hypocritically call out the sins of the laity while failing to confront those of leadership. A biblical example of this is the woman caught in adultery (John 8:3–11). The scribes and Pharisees brought the woman to stand before everyone and challenged Jesus by quoting the law that she should be stoned. Jesus wrote on the ground without answering them. When they persisted for an answer, he told them to let the one who has no sin be the first to cast a stone at the woman. Jesus began writing on the ground again. After hearing that, one by one, they left, beginning with the older ones. The one person who could have condemned her did not. Instead, Jesus told the woman to go and sin no more. Why did they bring this woman and not the man also? The Bible does not say, but it takes two people to commit adultery.

Removing the Dirt in the Church

The Bible does say that they were trying to test Jesus so they could charge him with going against the law. They were trying to use this woman as an object lesson to put Jesus in his place and preserve their sense of authority. Only they were the ones who needed correcting.

Leaders in the church are not the only ones who can be swift to judge the sins of others. This can also manifest in laity being prone to point out every so-called flaw in leadership while overlooking shortcomings among congregants. Some churches tend to keep the pastor and leadership under a microscope, pressuring them to abide by their personal preferences or traditions. Only in these cases, sin is not really the issue in the leadership. The people are sinning as they attempt to control the pastor as one controls a puppet. Sadly, many churches eventually split over control issues. Battle lines are drawn over things that have nothing to do with sin against God. Situations like these are a poor representation of Christ and his church.

One final problem in the church system that we will briefly consider is the sin of partiality. This was a problem in the early church almost at its onset. Early church community was described as follows:

> And the congregation of those who believed were of one heart and soul; and not one of them claimed that anything belonging to him was his own, but all things were common property to them. And with great power the apostles were giving testimony to the resurrection of the Lord Jesus, and abundant grace was upon them all. For there was not a needy person among them, for all who were owners of land or houses would sell them and bring the proceeds of the sales and lay them at the apostles' feet, and they would be distributed to each as any had need. (Acts 4:32–35)

By Acts 6:1, things looked different:

> Now at this time while the disciples were increasing in number, a complaint arose on the part of the Hellenistic Jews against the native Hebrews, because their widows were being overlooked in the daily serving of food.

Down and Dirty

Hellenistic Jews were Greek-speaking Jews who were likely born outside of Palestine, perhaps due to the Diaspora, and who had returned and settled in Jerusalem. The early church went from sharing all things in common and everyone having what they needed to some of the widows being neglected. To their credit, however, this complaint was taken seriously and quickly resolved. The people were instructed to choose seven qualified men to handle the food distribution, which they did.

James, in chapter 2 of his epistle to the scattered saints, warned against showing partiality to the rich and of dishonoring the poor among them (James 2:1–6). He reminded them of the royal law, "You shall love your neighbor as yourself (James 2:8)." And admonished them that showing partiality is sin (James 2:9).

Sadly, partiality is alive and well in the church today. It is seen in both partiality to the rich and in favoritism of one race or ethnic group over another. If we don't do better, heaven may be culture shock for some. Heaven will be very diverse.

> After these things I looked, and behold, a great multitude which no one could count, from every nation and all tribes and peoples and tongues, standing before the throne and before the Lamb, clothed in white robes, and palm branches were in their hands; and they cry out with a loud voice, saying, "Salvation to our God who sits on the throne, and to the Lamb." (Revelation 7:9–10)

It was God's plan all along for all the nations to worship him together. God told Abraham that all the nations of the earth would be blessed through his seed (Genesis 12:3, 18:18, 22:18; Acts 3:25; Galatians 3:8). The seed of Abraham was referring to Christ (Galatians 3:16). Paul makes it very clear in Galatians 3:28–29 that we are one in Christ and that all other ways that we classify ourselves do not supersede that oneness in Christ.

God takes the sin of partiality very seriously. "For judgment will be merciless to one who has shown no mercy" (James 2:13). Those who practice the sin of partiality are not showing mercy, which is like asking God to be merciless toward them. Unfortunately, in the United States and other places, the Bible was misused and taken out of context to justify an

Removing the Dirt in the Church

unbiblical slavery that is still bearing the fruit of ethnic partiality in the church today.

God is not pleased with partiality for any reason. It fails to acknowledge God as creator of all men and that all men are made in his image (James 3:9). God expects us to put some action with our blessings of those who are truly less fortunate by giving them what they need (James 2:15–16). It is one of the marks of true religion (James 1:27). To neglect to do so when able is sin (James 2:9).

Sin is messy. Left unchecked it will wreak havoc in the church just as a hurricane does the cities in its path. But the church is filled with people who are all in different stages of spiritual growth. How does the ideal church look? What can one realistically expect from relationships within the church? We will answer these questions as we explore God's dirt removal plan.

PART 3

God's Dirt Removal Plan

This section will show how God's intended design for cleansing the church includes, in addition to individual surrender to him and his Word, a godly relationship with one another according to his Word.

The Body of Christ

The church is referred to in the Bible as the body of Christ. There is one body (Ephesians 4:4) of which Christ is the head and Savior (Ephesians 5:23). Paul gave a description of some gifts in the body, their function, and goals in Ephesians 4:11–16:

> And He gave some as apostles, and some as prophets, and some as evangelists, and some as pastors and teachers, for the equipping of the saints for the work of service, to the building up of the body of Christ; until we all attain to the unity of the faith, and of the knowledge of the Son of God, to a mature man, to the measure of the stature which belongs to the fullness of Christ. As a result, we are no longer to be children, tossed here and there by waves and carried about by every wind of doctrine, by the trickery of men, by craftiness in deceitful scheming; but speaking the truth in love, we are to grow up in all aspects into Him

Removing the Dirt in the Church

who is the head, even Christ, from whom the whole
body, being fitted and held together by what every
joint supplies, according to the proper working of each
individual part, causes the growth of the body for the
building up of itself in love.

In the Scripture passage above, we see that the apostles, prophets,
evangelists, pastors, and teachers were given to equip the saints for the
work of service and for the building up of the body of Christ. The saints
need to be equipped. The body of Christ needs to be built up. This work is
to continue until we all attain the unity of the faith and the knowledge of
the Son of God. The church is the place to be to attain unity of the faith
and knowledge of the Son of God. The result will be maturity in Christ,
and no longer being easily deceived by deceitful people who speak false
doctrine. Instead, we will speak the truth in love and grow up in all aspects
into Christ. It is important to understand that Christ formed the parts of
the body to be interdependent. By what means does Christ choose to fit
and hold the body together? By what every joint supplies! According to
what? According to the proper working of each individual part! We need
one another! Each individual working as intended by Christ is what causes
the growth of the body to build itself up in love. Christ builds up his body
through its individual members, who speak the truth in love and properly
function as he has gifted them.

Paul again describes this interdependency in 1 Corinthians 12:14–27:

For the body is not one member, but many. If the foot
says, "Because I am not a hand, I am not a part of the
body," it is not for this reason any the less a part of the
body. And if the ear says, "Because I am not an eye,
I am not a part of the body," it is not for this reason
any the less a part of the body. If the whole body were
an eye, where would the hearing be? If the whole were
hearing, where would the sense of smell be? But now God
has placed the members, each one of them, in the body,
just as He desired. If they were all one member, where
would the body be? But now there are many members,

God's Dirt Removal Plan

but one body. And the eye cannot say to the hand, "I have no need of you"; or again the head to the feet, "I have no need of you." On the contrary, it is much truer that the members of the body which seem to be weaker are necessary; and those members of the body which we deem less honorable, on these we bestow more abundant honor, and our less presentable members become much more presentable, whereas our more presentable members have no need of it. But God has so composed the body, giving more abundant honor to that member which lacked, so that there may be no division in the body, but that the members may have the same care for one another. And if one member suffers, all the members suffer with it; if one member is honored, all the members rejoice with it. Now you are Christ's body, and individually members of it.

Just as the parts of a human body work together to accomplish things, such as provide nourishment, protect from harm, reach a destination, etc., the body of Christ also works together for the glory of God. It would be great if working together as the body of Christ came as naturally as blinking your eye to clear microscopic debris. You do not have to think about it. Your eye blinks reflexively. But unity within the body of Christ is not an instinctual process. The church is full of individuals who are at various stages of spiritual growth, and everyone varies in their ability to be consistent in their walk with Christ. It is no wonder, then, that things can get messy in the church. This is why we need instruction.

It is helpful to understand how we as individuals are all the same, and how we differ. We are all made in the image of God (Genesis 1:27); we were all born in sin (Romans 5:12) and are saved the same way, by grace through faith (Ephesians 2:8, 9); we were created for good works (Ephesians 2:10); and we were created by God for God's glory (Revelation 4:11). We are different by design, male and female (Genesis 1:27), and by gifting (1 Corinthians 12:14–20). When we see ourselves and others accurately, we can humbly adjust our expectations and responses accordingly. The epistles in the New Testament are replete with "one another" Scriptures that

73

Removing the Dirt in the Church

describe or command how Christians are to interact with each other. Since it does not come naturally for us, we must be instructed. Here are just ten:

ONE ANOTHER SCRIPTURES	
Romans 13:8-10	Love one another
1 Corinthians 12:25	Have the same care for one another
Ephesians 4:32	Forgive one another
Philippians 2:3-7	Esteem others as more important
Romans 15:7	Accept one another
James 5:16	Confess your sins to one another
Colossians 3:12-13	Bear with one another and forgive one another
Hebrews 10:25	Encourage one another
Colossians 3:9	Do not lie to one another
James 5:9	Do not complain against one another

Remember, Christ is the head of the body. Once we have confessed that Jesus is the Son of God, God is in us, and we are in him (1 John 4:15). We can do all that Christ commands us through the grace he gives us.

We're in This Together

What about all this dirt (sin) in the church? It's not supposed to be this way! This disappointment with dirt in the church is understandable when we are thinking about the church's objective. Dirt in the church shows us that we have not reached the goal yet. From another perspective, we need not be surprised by dirt in the church. Each individual is growing to maturity, which is a process. Furthermore, those considered mature have not reached perfection. This does not mean that we should have a laissez-faire attitude about sin within the body of Christ. To the contrary, it should call us to action. Often in the New Testament, it was problems with sin and immaturity in the local church that prompted an epistle to be written. The sins of divisiveness and failure to deal with blatant sin in the church at Corinth is what prompted Paul to write 1 Corinthians. They needed to be instructed.

In the twenty-first century, we have the advantage of the completed

God's Dirt Removal Plan

canon of Scripture. First-century Christians did not have that luxury. That fact, however, does not mean that twenty-first-century Christians will never have to deal with sin or immaturity in the local church. The day one becomes a follower of Christ, that new Christian is not downloaded with all knowledge needed to follow Christ in one day. New believers are indwelled with power and capacity, but it takes time to learn, practice, and grow to maturity. Both mature and immature people can sin against and hurt others. This is a fact that cannot be avoided. Therefore, we are commanded to be reconciled to one another, to forgive one another, and to bear with one another. The Christian who is impatient with an immature Christian is also displaying immaturity. These situations are opportunities for iron to sharpen iron (Proverbs 27:17), and for the grace which we have been given to be granted to others (Ephesians 4:29).

Both mature and immature people can sin against and hurt others. This is a fact that cannot be avoided.

After reading 1 Thessalonians 1, one may conclude that the church in Thessalonica was an ideal church. They demonstrated the positive cycle of evangelism. After hearing the word preached to them with full conviction by Paul (1 Thessalonians 1:5), they received it (1 Thessalonians 1:6). They became imitators of Paul, Silvanus, and Timothy (1 Thessalonians 1:6); became examples to others (1 Thessalonians 1:7); and finally sounded forth the word with conviction to others (1 Thessalonians 1:8). They "turned to God from idols to serve a living and true God" (1 Thessalonians 1:9).

In 1 Thessalonians 2, Paul certainly modeled the love and care ideal for leaders to have for those under their care. He did not flatter the people to loosen their pockets or win the favor of men (1 Thessalonians 2:5–6). He gently cared for them like a nursing mother would her children (1 Thessalonians 2:7). He gave them the gospel and gave himself to their spiritual growth (1 Thessalonians 2:8). He exemplified devout, upright, and blameless behavior toward them (1 Thessalonians 2:10). He exhorted,

Removing the Dirt in the Church

encouraged, and implored them to walk worthy of God as a father would his own children (1 Thessalonians 2:11–12). Paul acknowledged their suffering and persecution for the sake of Christ (1 Thessalonians 2:14). He longed to come and make sure they were not disturbed by the afflictions they were suffering, and when he could not, he chose to send Timothy to minister to them although he would be left alone (1 Thessalonians 3:1–3). Paul put the care and concern for these new believers above his own personal comfort. Who would not want a pastor like that?

Even in an ideal church, however, conditions may arise which require tough love to be exercised. For example, Paul commanded in his first letter to the church in Thessalonica that they were "to make it your ambition to lead a quiet life and attend to your own business and work with your hands" (1 Thessalonians 4:11). In his second letter, he instructed that if a man did not work, he should not eat (2 Thessalonians 3:10–12). While that may sound harsh to some, these instructions were indicated because there were people who thought Jesus would return at any time, so they stopped investing time and effort into the things necessary to sustain life. As a result, they became an unnecessary burden to others within the church. In this instance, the nonworkers were taking advantage (perhaps unintentionally) of others in the church. And the people who were feeding them were (possibly inadvertently) enabling irresponsible behavior. Misunderstandings can happen. This is why we are to be patient with one another as we learn to properly apply the Word of God to our lives. It is a process.

It is not uncommon for Christians to sin. While it shouldn't be deliberate, it happens. Conscientious Christians often immediately self-correct when they sin because the Holy Spirit convicts them. They are intentionally living to please God and intentionally with haste putting away sin from their lives as soon as they become aware of it. When we are blind to our own faults, that's when God uses others within the body of Christ to help get us back on track. Matthew 18:15–17 outlines this process:

> "If your brother sins, go and show him his fault in private;
> if he listens to you, you have won your brother. But if he
> does not listen to you, take one or two more with you, so

God's Dirt Removal Plan

that by the mouth of two or three witnesses every fact may
be confirmed. If he refuses to listen to them, tell it to the
church; and if he refuses to listen even to the church, let
him be to you as a Gentile and a tax collector.

Speaking to your brother in private means that we are not needlessly
exposing the sin of someone. We are to approach them in gentleness with
the goal of restoration (Galatians 6:1). It is only after a Christian brother
refuses to turn away from their sin to God that you involve someone else
(two or three witnesses) and subsequently the church if they persist in
sinful behavior. It is unfortunate that much sin remains in local churches
as they neglect to follow this biblical instruction on discipline within the
church.

Failure to exercise biblical discipline manifests in several ways. The
"silence is golden" approach allows sin to go unchecked. It is as if sin
is OK to practice because no one will say or do anything about it. The
failure to confront sin may be motivated from a fear of confrontation.
It's not popular to insert yourself in the "choices" of others in this day
and age. Failure to confront may also be due to an "everybody's doing
it" atmosphere. If sin is rampant in a local body of believers, it may seem
hopeless to confront it. Whereas the opposite extreme wants to deal
with sin at all costs without the humble and meek attitude outlined in
Scripture. This becomes just as sinful as the sin that is being opposed.
Even Jesus did not come into the world to condemn the world (John
3:17). Those who are quick to condemn are often hypocritical, which is
condemned in Scripture (Matthew 5:1–3). Another problem is failure
to follow through to the end of the discipline process. For example,
one may humbly and privately approach their erring brother to restore
them, but then drop the matter completely if they fail to repent. It can
be discouraging when it seems like you care more about someone else's
spiritual life than they do. You may, but pray, trust God, and follow the
process through. Approaches that fail to do so all fall short of God's
glory as they are ineffective in removing sin from the church.

The ideal church, then, is one where people have latitude to grow.
It is to be an environment that lavishes with grace yet loves enough
to confront sin out of concern for the offender. It is one centered

Removing the Dirt in the Church

around Christ and his Word—not the preferences or traditions of men (Matthew 15:9). It is one where people who see deviations from Christ and his Word will, after humble self-examination, lovingly speak up and confront others to effect change for God's glory (Galatians 6:1). It is one where the wounded are lovingly cared for and uplifted (1 Thessalonians 5:14). It is one of mutual accountability for leaders and laity alike (1 Timothy 5:19–21). But this environment will not be attained if there is one standard for some but not for all. It will not be accomplished if false doctrine or misapplication of Scripture is not confronted. It will not be realized if people bury their heads in the sand concerning sin and no one speaks up.

Each person in the church bears some responsibility in the culture of the local church. What is your contribution? Are you intentional about your personal growth as a Christian? If not, you may be depriving the body of what God intends for you to contribute. Are you one who complains about things gone wrong but offers no solutions or even prayers for resolving the problem? If so, you may be a destructive force instead of building up the body. What about serving? Are you allowing past hurts to keep you from being involved with the local church? Your perspective may be the very thing that helps facilitate the needed change. We must not forget that Christ is the head of the church, but he often uses people to accomplish his will. Christ, his Word, and his will must be the church's central focus. Mutual accountability without partiality are also key components to God's dirt removal plan. The Word of Christ must be lived out in the individual lives of his body, the church.

Are you surrendered to Christ? If not, make that your first order of business. Do you know what the Bible actually teaches? Become a Bible student for life. You will never exhaust its truths but will certainly grow when you rightly apply them. Do you share your life with others? Do you allow others to share their lives with you? When functioning as designed, the body of Christ is alive and connected, building itself up in love. It receives nourishment, eliminates wastes, grows to maturity, and continues its mission to make disciples of Christ. We are in this together.

My Survivor Story of Clergy Sexual Abuse

Warning: Survivors of clergy sexual abuse may be triggered by reading this section. If necessary, you may skip to the paragraph starting with "a word to the survivor of any clergy abuse."

In this final section, I'd like to share a case study that highlights a modern-day example of dirt in the church and God's redemptive power at work in the hearts of the repentant. In an ideal world, everyone who represented God could be trusted to accurately do so. We live, however, in a fallen world where that is simply not the case. People in authority have the capacity to abuse their authority. This is also true in the Christian church. I know because I am a survivor of clergy sexual abuse. I am sharing my testimony because many people are not aware that there is such a thing as clergy sexual abuse of adult victims. My prayer is that my story will be used by God to raise awareness of clergy sexual abuse so that churches will do more to hold clergy accountable and not blame the victim(s) as so many churches have done. I pray that my story inspires parents not to manipulate their children, as that makes it easy for them to be manipulated by abusers—and to intentionally teach their children to think for themselves, to make wise choices, and to recognize if someone is trying to manipulate them. I also pray to help other survivors of abuse to understand that God loves you and that there is hope for your future. Here is my story:

Very early in our marriage, one of the ministers on staff at our church and his wife befriended my husband and me. They were more than ten years our senior. It all began one day as we were sharing a meal. I expressed that as a married woman, I had avoided having male friends to protect our marriage from infidelity. The minister then expressed that I should "stick with" him. I took that to mean that he would be a safe friend, like an older brother or father figure that I could trust. I ignored my feelings of discomfort and trusted that because he was a minister and that he knew better than I that I'd be safe having a friendship with him. He began to call me on a regular basis. I was somewhat isolated at that time, so I welcomed adult conversation as a blessing. I also assumed that since our spouses were aware of the

Removing the Dirt in the Church

conversations and did not verbalize any objections to me, that the friendship must be "OK." It was during these conversations that what I now understand to be the grooming process began. He primarily used special treatment, secrets, and philosophical discussions to groom me for sexual abuse, and he used his knowledge of "what God wanted" to control me. He knew me well enough to know that pleasing God was what I wanted more than anything, and he used that desire to please God to his personal advantage.

Initially, the conversations made me feel like a real adult. He was the first minister of that age who allowed me to call him by his first name. We were "friends," so why not? Special treatment #1: I was the only young woman that I knew of that he befriended in this way. I especially appreciated being treated like an adult by someone more than ten years my senior because I had a more youthful face than my age. As a result, I was often treated like a child by more experienced adults, which was a source of frustration for me. I felt accepted by him.

During these conversations, we talked about a variety of topics. In addition to general conversation, we eventually talked about various childhood experiences, some of which were traumatic. Special treatment #2: The fact that he shared traumatic events from his childhood with me made the friendship seem mutual, like he trusted or needed me to be his friend instead of him only being there for me as a big brother or father figure. His trusting me made me feel like I was his equal, which I found very affirming. Secret #1: He asked me to keep the events he shared with me between us. I also shared my strained relationship with my father with him. He proved to be a good listener and seemed genuinely interested in my well-being.

Philosophical discussion: Early in the friendship, he introduced a hypothetical scenario for our discussion. He asserted that if a spouse ever committed adultery, and the innocent spouse was unaware of it, that it would be wrong for the adulterer to tell them. He stated that the adulterer would only be attempting to assuage their guilty conscience and that it would be unloving to dump their guilt on the unsuspecting spouse. I disagreed and stated that I would want to know if something like that ever happened, and that I would confess if I ever did something like that. At the time, however, I did not think

God's Dirt Removal Plan

that anything remotely close to adultery could happen to me. (I do not like using the word adultery to describe clergy sexual abuse because it implies consent. I'll explain more later.)

Special treatment #3: On occasion, we would have lunch together. It was during these times when we spoke in person that he began to get physical. He'd try to hug and kiss me inappropriately after taking me home. We were used to hugging at church, but this was different. I'd push him off me, and he'd apologize. Secret #2: He convinced me not to tell anyone that he had attempted to hug and kiss me inappropriately because he said he'd lose his ministry if anyone found out. He convinced me to continue in the friendship for the sake of his ministry. God would want me to forgive him.

To my own detriment, I kept his secrets. Over time, his attempting to get physical, my pushing him away, and his apologizing became a cycle. I was completely unprepared for that situation. I went over my own behavior in my mind to ensure that I did not do anything to lead him on. I didn't dress in a special way or put on lipstick. I never verbally expressed any desire to be physical with him. To the contrary, I wanted him to be proud of my husband and me. I never felt in danger of committing adultery because I knew I was committed to my own husband. I was confused as to what God required of me as far as forgiveness was concerned. To make matters more complicated, I was unprepared for the physiological responses of my own body. I did not love him in that way, but my reaction time of pushing him away began to get slower. He was beginning to wear me down. I didn't want to be physical with him, but I felt like I was trapped. The friendship was mostly pleasant, especially the conversations, but I didn't know how to stop his advances.

Once after we had eaten out, he asked me to come to his house. We were on the porch talking. He asked me to come inside, and he promised me that he would not try anything inappropriate. I didn't want to go inside, but I also didn't want to end the conversation. And it did seem wise from a safety perspective to go inside. I figured he knew his neighborhood better than I did. But it was on that occasion that despite his promise, he attempted to get physical again, and I froze. I felt trapped. If I had screamed, his secret would be out, as there were others in the house.

81

Removing the Dirt in the Church

He then did what he wanted to do to me. I didn't understand what was happening at the time, but I experienced a dissociative state, which is a type of response of the body to trauma. It felt like an out-of-body experience. It was as if I were frozen, helplessly watching what was happening to me. I laid there and internally prayed that he would stop and come to his senses. He stopped and began to cry, "What have I done? Have I lost my ministry?" I assured him I would not tell what "we" had done. Instead of being angry at him for breaking his promise not to be inappropriate, I was comforting him and promising once again to keep his secret. I had been successfully groomed and controlled.

I was relieved and thankful for what appeared to be genuine repentance. I thought that his stopping meant that he had finally come to his senses and that my prayers had been answered, but that was not the case! As reality set in, I felt shock and disgust. He had used me like an object! I feel like I was mentally, emotionally, and spiritually raped. Instead of using a gun, the Scriptures that I love were twisted and used as handcuffs to render me helpless. I learned the hard way that I needed to take matters into my own hands. I made a decision to never be alone with him again. Unfortunately, he convinced me that it was unfair of me to make that decision without discussing it with him.

When we were supposed to be discussing the boundaries of the friendship, it happened again, and I experienced another traumatic response during which I reasoned that I must be in love with him. I mean, I'm not the kind of person that just casually has sex with friends or with anyone other than my husband. Concluding that I was in love with him was the only thing that my brain could come up with to make sense of what was happening. I am filled with regret about the things I did while in that state of mind. There is more I could say about my own ignorance and his taking advantage of me, but I believe I've given sufficient background of the circumstances.

I was not in love with him, and I never allowed myself to be alone with him again. I didn't realize until months later that he really didn't want our friendship to be platonic. He kept inviting me to be alone with him. I'd had enough and finally got the courage to tell my husband what had happened. Upon my husband's insistence, I also told the minister's wife—only to find out that he had done this before. To add insult to injury, he lied to our spouses about how things happened. Some friend he turned out to be.

Clergy sexual abuse is not an affair (Garland 2013). It can happen to people of all ages, colors, and educational backgrounds. It is different from an adulterous affair because of the authority of the clergy. Consent cannot be given when one person is in authority over the other. That is why in the Bible David, Hophni, and Phinehas all committed abuse against the women they had exploitative sex with. Bathsheba was portrayed as a little ewe lamb by Nathan the prophet to David when he confronted him for his sin. What power does a little ewe lamb have over a powerful king? Hophni and Phinehas were priests who should have been teaching the women the ways of God instead of exploiting them. Furthermore, clergy sexual abuse is generally abusive in nature due to the coercion and manipulation involved. Merriam-Webster's full definition of adultery is as follows: "voluntary sexual intercourse between a married person and someone other than that person's current spouse or partner" (2020). Manipulation and coercion are types of force which, by definition, means the person who was coerced and/or manipulated did not volunteer, thus making the word adultery an inappropriate descriptor of clergy sexual abuse. In my case, my desire to please God was used against me. My choices as I understood them were to cause a ministry to end or to forgive, keep silent, and continue a friendship—or to be unloving and selfish instead of keeping silent. Although I know better now, at the time I didn't think I had any good choices.

While it is unquestionably unethical and inappropriate for a professor to be sexually involved with a student or for a professional counselor to be sexually involved with a client, even more so it is sinful, unethical, and inappropriate for clergy to be sexually involved with a parishioner. No clergy is powerless over the temptation to exploit the vulnerabilities of their parishioner(s). Many people do not understand the psychological, spiritual, and emotional dynamics involved in clergy sexual abuse and insist on calling it adultery. Even other victims call it adultery. No matter what it's called, it's definitely different from cases involving two people of equal power. There is a growing body of research available on the topic. Please educate yourself.

Removing the Dirt in the Church

My hope is that everyone who hears my story will come to understand this type of abuse, do all in their power to prevent it, and respond to cases of clergy sexual abuse in ways that do not blame or further abuse the victim. It is equally important that they strictly hold the abuser accountable, preventing them from repeating abuse. It's a messy situation but keeping up appearances is not important to God. Judging a righteous judgment is important to God (John 7:24). Some may think that exposing clergy sexual abuse makes God look bad. It does not. It confirms that we are all under God's authority and accountable to him for our actions. No one gets a free pass. Exposing abuse by members of the clergy actually gives glory to God. We can give God glory in more ways than doing everything right. We also give glory to God when we agree with God and call sin what it is—sin. Remember in the character study on Achan that he gave God glory when he finally confessed his sin. Had he confessed on his own, he may have had a different outcome. When the church and its leaders cover up clergy sexual abuse, they are asking God to expose them, much like God exposed Achan. The consequences of his sin affected all those around him. For the health of the church at large, expose and deal with this sin. God is more concerned with the way things are than the way things look. God does not want us to merely look holy. He wants us to be holy! And judgment must begin at the house of God (1 Peter 4:17)! It is only through seeing our sin, calling it what it is, and bringing it to the cross of Christ that we can be cleansed and made whole (1 John 1:9).

A word to parents. A compliant child is not the goal of parenting. The goal of a Christian parent is to bring children up in the nurture and admonition of the Lord (Ephesians 6:4). Some parents use an authoritarian parenting style which emphasizes obedience to the parent to the exclusion of teaching the child how to think for themselves. We do our children a disservice when we do all their thinking for them. It is appropriate for parents to do the thinking for babies and toddlers, but as the child develops, so should the opportunity and freedom to learn to think for themselves. It is a skill to be taught by giving them opportunities to think for themselves with guidance. When we manipulate them by withholding affection unless they are completely

84

God's Dirt Removal Plan

compliant, we are emotionally abusing them, which paves the way for them to be abused by others. The Bible does instruct children to obey their parents (Ephesians 6:1). But parents are to bring their children up to be capable adults, which means children should know how to evaluate circumstances and make wise choices before they leave home as an adult. Some children are more compliant by nature than others. Parents may need to deliberately give compliant children tough choices to make. Teach them that they are responsible for their own choices and actions. Also teach them they are not responsible for the choices and actions of others. Teach them when it is appropriate from the Bible's perspective to disobey authority. Teach them that God is pleased when he is honored above men. Listen to your children. Affirm and encourage sound thought processes. Don't let the first time they feel heard by an adult be from someone who is trying to groom them for abuse. Prepare them for the world they live in.

A word to the survivor of any type of clergy abuse. Dear survivor, what happened to you is not your fault. The person holding the office of clergy should have been trustworthy to watch for your soul—not abuse you. If you feel that my story of clergy sexual abuse was worse than yours, do not minimize your experience. Please glean everything you can from your experience. If you feel that your story was worse than mine, please do not conclude that your case is hopeless. God can work for good everything that was meant for evil. And his grace is sufficient for you too. Do not be deceived. God still loves you. God's plan to use you for his glory, which he had before the foundation of the world, has not been voided. God's sovereignty includes redeeming every misuse and abuse. The person who abused you sinned against you and against God. Vengeance belongs to God (Romans 12:19). Do not allow your pain and hurt caused by someone in the church to keep you away from the church. While you may need to find a local congregation that is not spiritually toxic, the church is a body of believers that minister grace to one another. God's grace ministered to you through mature godly believers is healing for your soul. The church would also be robbed of your ability, as you are able, to bring wisdom and comfort that you have received from God as a survivor. Ask God to make you better and not bitter because of what you've been through. Ask him to make you whole

85

Removing the Dirt in the Church

again. You are still here. You can make a difference. Make your time count. See and trust God for who he is and do not allow your difficulties to make him small in your eyes. Just because the person in your life who was supposed to be representing God could not be trusted, that does not mean that God cannot be trusted. Dare to trust God and allow him to have his way in your life.

I was very young and naive when I was abused. I was the typical trusting naive type (a label used in the book *Safe People* (Cloud and Townsend 1996)). I didn't think something like nonconsensual, coercive sex could happen to me. I was oblivious to the danger of disregarding my own inner reservations. I trusted too much in him as a minister of God and not enough in the Holy Spirit who dwells in me. I was right all along about the wisdom of avoiding special opposite-sex friendships, especially in that season of immaturity. I, however, was especially primed for this abuse as I was born the child of a minister. Personal sacrifices in the name of ministry were a way of life for my family. Having accepted Christ as a young child, my heart was to please God, but I had not learned to think critically for myself, especially in spiritual matters. I was reared to obey authority without question. In my world, obeying daddy was obeying God. I thought I knew enough not to follow authority into blatant evil, but the fact that I considered that member of the clergy to be a friend who had my best interest at heart clouded my judgment. He had demonstrated that he was not really my friend, but I sincerely thought I was following the golden rule by giving him more and more chances. I thought I was forgiving him seventy times seven as commanded in the Scriptures (Matthew 18:21–22). I wrongly believed that forgiveness practically meant living as though the offense never happened. I didn't hear people in authority tell others they were sorry much growing up. It was even more rare, if ever, for me to hear an adult apologize to a child. When the minister apologized to me, each time, it seemed heartfelt. I thought the right thing to do was to just let it go and get back to the friendship. I didn't know that I, a Christian, could reject someone's friendship and still be pleasing to God. At the times when I should have been angry at him violating

86

God's Dirt Removal Plan

me, I was being manipulated to protect him. I could have forgiven him without continuing to put myself in harm's way. I did eventually deny him access to me. But I wish I had done it after the first attempt of inappropriate behavior. I now understand that I am not obligated to restore a relationship with someone who has a pattern of sinning against me who has not demonstrated the fruit of repentance. Many people can charm through speech, saying everything in a convincing manner. I realize that I should have looked at his actions to see if he was living like he was sorry. Moreover, I understand now that I would not have been responsible for the consequences that he may have faced had I reported him for sexually harassing me. I didn't even understand that I was being sexually harassed. This happened before the internet and widespread training on the subject.

I'm truly grateful for the grace extended to me by God and my husband. And I'm grateful that the blood of Jesus covers the shame of my ignorance.

I don't blame God for what happened to me because had I understood and listened to his guidance this would not have happened. Being a mature Christian takes more than just being sincere. It takes a renewed mind that can properly understand and apply the Scriptures to daily life. Learning to follow the Holy Spirit's guidance above all other voices is a lesson I've learned the hard way. I've also learned that spiritual authority has boundaries. Clergy do not have the authority to tell parishioners how to specifically carry out God's plan for them. That is the Holy Spirit's job. They are to rightly expound the Scriptures and allow the Holy Spirit to give the specifics. I am to study for myself, searching the Scriptures to see if what is said is properly interpreted, and then I am to apply the Scriptures to my life by the grace that God gives me. I didn't want or ask for clergy sexual abuse to happen to me, but we live in a fallen world where wicked and evil men misuse the power of their position and twist the Word of God for their unholy lusts. Every person in the church is not a Christian, and no one, Christian or not, is to be blindly followed.

Removing the Dirt in the Church

My experience of clergy sexual abuse does not define who I am. My relationship with Christ defines me. I have learned that it is the accuser and enemy of my soul who wants to make me feel that I am too ignorant to be used by God, or that I should sit in the corner filled with shame and disgrace for the rest of my life. Christ says otherwise. When I see Christ for who he is, then I can have confidence that he can cleanse, forgive, teach, and use anybody. His holiness is transferred to my account, and I cannot tarnish it. I was not saved as a child and then left to keep myself by my own diligent effort to obey God. My performance record is not what keeps me. His performance record keeps me. Despite being ignorant to my own detriment in my past, Christ has given me his mind. I have the mind of Christ! My past does not define me; however, it has served as a catalyst for me to learn to discern for myself. My love for personal Bible study, learning to rightly divide the Word of God for myself, was fueled even more by my abuse experience.

God has freed me to share my story. I know that no one is better or worse than me. The ground is level at the cross, and we all need Jesus! Now God is using me to teach others to rightly divide the Word of truth for themselves. God reveals himself, his will, and his general plan for our lives through his Word. I am grateful for this opportunity to let you know that no matter what you have done, or what has been done to you, there is hope for you in Christ and his Word. Trust him today!

Reflections

1. How have you handled being mistreated by untrustworthy people? Ask God to draw you closer to him.
2. How has your relationship with God been affected because of the various trials in your life? Ask for God's help to strengthen your faith no matter what.
3. What can you do to cultivate greater spiritual growth and dependence upon God? Ask God to help you to do those things intentionally and consistently.

God's Dirt Removal Plan

Prayer

Gracious heavenly Father, you are so awesome! You can take whatever difficulty I face and make it an opportunity for me to grow in maturity and in closer fellowship with you. I am never without hope because of you! Thank you for using the trauma in my life to glorify your name. Your redeeming power is unfathomable. May I continue to learn, grow in your grace, and give you glory for as long as I have breath. I love you because you loved me first. I am grateful beyond words. Please do above and beyond what I ask or think for your glory according to your power working in me. In the name of Jesus Christ, I pray. Amen.

Conclusion

For the majority of my adult life, I have struggled with driving the speed limit. I tend to go over unless I have the cruise control set for the limit. I often feel the Holy Spirit's conviction when I catch myself speeding because the Bible teaches that we are to obey the laws of the land, which includes the speed limit. I appreciate having cruise control, so I don't have to think about whether I'm speeding or not. Similarly, I have inwardly wished that by the flip of a switch the Holy Spirit could be set to automatically control my thoughts, words, and actions. We have seen that it does not work that way. We must intentionally surrender to God. Loving God with my heart, soul, mind, and strength necessitates using my mind to think, speak, and act biblically—to intentionally surrender to him. Also, we must know what his will is before we can surrender to it. Thus, knowing how to study God's Word, while accurately interpreting and applying it, is also paramount.

It is my hope that *Removing the Dirt in the Church* has shed light on both the normalcy of dirt in the church and the necessity of intentional surrender to God and relational work within the body of Christ to remove it. We need not be shocked at the sin of people in the church, but we must actively work to remove it. In brief character studies, we saw both the consequences of those who disobeyed God and how God's grace enabled those who had previously failed him to be used for God's glory. When those who are disillusioned with the church lower their expectations of others and raise their expectations of God working in them, both to grow in maturity themselves and to help others do the same, then they will see God's dirt removal plan in action. Understanding that growth happens over time can help us receive grace and also give it to others. It is a delicate balance of being sure the log has been removed from our own eyes, and then a willingness to assist our brother with removing the speck from his

91

eye (Matthew 7:3–5). The body of Christ was made to work together to care for itself by God's grace.

A word to anyone reading this book who has avoided Christianity due to all the "hypocrites" in the church: Please reconsider. God's plan of salvation is the same for everyone. We are saved by grace through faith. There is no substitute for trust in the death, burial, and resurrection of Christ to save and keep one from sin. Don't allow others' spiritual immaturity or being a counterfeit keep you from the riches of God's grace toward you. Christ died and rose again for your sins. You will not reach the perfection you yearn for apart from God. Heaven is real, but you will only get there God's way after this life is over. Will you come to him and surrender to him and live with the integrity that you longed to see in the church—and take your place within a local body of believers in Christ?

God's grace is sufficient for all. No matter what you have done or what's been done to you, God is able to redeem you and use you for his glory. Let go of unbelief, pain, and regret. Dare to trust and believe the love that God has for you. Accept his provision for your salvation from sin through the death, burial, and resurrection of his Son, Jesus Christ. It's the best decision you will ever make. Then love him back by living a life fully surrendered to him.

REFERENCES

Cloud, Henry, and John Townsend. 1996. *Safe People: How to Find Relationships That Are Good for You and Avoid Those That Aren't.* Grand Rapids, MI: Zondervan.

de Weger, Stephen E. "Clerical Sexual Misconduct Involving Adults within the Roman Catholic Church." PhD diss., Queensland University of Technology, 2016. https://eprints.qut.edu.au/96038/.

Garland, Diana. "When Wolves Wear Shepherds' Clothing: Helping Women Survive Clergy Sexual Abuse." *Journal of Religion & Abuse* 8, no 2 (2006): 37–70.

_____. "Don't Call It an Affair: Understanding and Preventing Clergy Sexual Misconduct with Adults." *Clergy Sexual Abuse* (2013): 118–43.

Harris, Robert L. 1980. *Theological Wordbook of the Old Testament.* Chicago: Moody Publishers.

Merriam-Webster. Definition of "Adultery." Accessed November 23, 2020. https://www.merriam-webster.com/dictionary/adultery.

Morey, Ann-Janine. "Blaming Women for the Sexually Abusive Male Pastor." *The Christian Century* 105, (1988): 866–69.

Pooler, David K. "Making Safe Places and Spaces: Voices of Survivors of Clergy Sexual Abuse." Paper presented at the Hope and Healing Conference, Buffalo, NY, 2017.

Short, Emily C. 2004. "Torts: Praying for the Parish or Preying on the Parish-Clergy Sexual Misconduct and the Tort of Clergy Malpractice." *Oklahoma Law Review* 57: 183.

Wayne, Luke. 2016. "How Do You Identify a False Teacher?" https://carm.org/other-questions/how-do-you-identify-a-false-teacher/.

ABOUT THE AUTHOR

Mary Smith became a follower of Christ at an early age. The daughter of a pastor, she loved singing in the choir and learning about the God of the Bible as a child. Her love for Christ, the Bible, and gospel music would grow with her into adulthood.

She met her husband, Raymond, in ninth grade at the school gospel choir rehearsal. They have been working together in music ministry since then; Mary, as a worship leader, singer, soloist, and choir director and Raymond, the director of music for their local church, as a worship leader, gifted pianist, and organist.

After her experience of clergy sexual abuse, Mary sought, without initial success, to experience the mentoring type of relationship commanded in Titus 2:3-5 of older women to teach the younger women. She now has a love and burden for women's ministry. *Removing the Dirt in the Church* contains many of the lessons that she has learned that she wished someone had taught her.

Mary E. Smith earned a master's degree from Wayne State University and is a certified Biblical counselor, Precept Ministries International Bible study leader, and Bible teacher. As a survivor of clergy sexual abuse, she has a unique frame of reference to many issues in the church today that are odious or injurious to God and people. Smith and her husband, Raymond, have three grown sons, several grandchildren, and live in Detroit, Michigan.